More Advance Praise for Nancy Azara's *Spirit Taking Form*

"Nancy Azara tells us how to meditate our way into our imaginations and give our thoughts and feelings visible form. Reading *Spirit Taking Form*, the life lessons of a pioneer feminist artist, could release the artist in each of us, and create a vision of art in which everyone matters."
—Gloria Steinem

"This charming, inspiring, and intimate book will gently tempt your spirit into taking—and making—some new forms."
—Phyllis Chesler, author of *Women and Madness, Woman's Inhumanity to Woman*, and *Women of the Wall: Claiming Sacred Ground at Judaism's Holy Site*

"In this beautiful book, Nancy Azara offers affirmation and pathways for nourishing the gift of authentic creative expression that lies within all of us. By sharing her deepest truths as an artist and her own journey out of fear and into union with her spiritual self, she inspires us to do the same. After reading her book, I found myself newly equipped, newly ready to follow my art spirit."
—Andrea Gilats, Split Rock Arts Program, University of Minnesota

"*Spirit Taking Form* is a self-empowerment guide that everyone, whether naturally inner or outer directed, may use to become more creative and integrated."
—Suzanne Iasenza, Ph.D., Psychologist

"In *Spirit Taking Form*, Nancy Azara offers us a gift of wisdom. She calls out to the artist in each of us, urging us to take risks in the realm of visual experience and guiding us with a sure hand. Her advice to students rings true because it is deeply grounded in a personal and spiritual quest."
—Berenice Malka Fisher, author of *No Angel in the Classroom: Teaching Through Feminist Discourse*

"Over the many years of her emergence as an important American sculptor, Azara has been following the subtle and ineffable paths of spirit, memory, and feeling, making stunning discoveries in the realms of the invisible and the imaginary... This book will take you on a similar journey to your own inner sites of wonder."
—Gloria F. Orenstein, author of *The Reflowering of the Goddess*

"Reads like a letter from a close friend. The stories lure you in. The meditational exercises inspire you to create personal images. This book is for everyone who wants to learn to experience the profound pleasure of artmaking."
—Mari Messer, author of *Pencil Dancing: New Ways to Free Your Creative Spirit*

"This fervent, meditative book is a gift. Through wonderfully designed exercises for the hand and mind, Nancy leads readers both inward toward personal sources of memory and imagination and outward toward the natural world. Turning these pages becomes a journey of discovery toward one's own wellsprings."
—Eleanor Munro, author of *Originals: American Woman Artists*

"It does not matter if you have ever studied art before, or if you are an accomplished artist. Azara's exercises and meditations will guide you adeptly into this arena. Her observations about and suggestions for cultivating imagination and visual memory are especially cogent."
—Deborah J. Haynes, Ph.D., author of *The Vocation of the Artist* and Professor and Chair, Department of Fine Arts, University of Colorado at Boulder.

Spirit
Taking
Form

MAKING A
SPIRITUAL PRACTICE
OF MAKING ART

Nancy Azara

Red Wheel
Boston, MA / York Beach, ME

To Darla Bjork, friend, companion,
fellow traveler over these many years.

First published in 2002 by
Red Wheel/Weiser, LLC
York Beach, ME
With offices at:
368 Congress Street
Boston, MA 02210
www.redwheelweiser.com

Library of Congress Cataloging-in-Publication Data

Azara, Nancy J., 1939–
    Spirit taking form : making a spiritual practice of making art/Nancy Azara.
        p. cm.
Includes bibliographical reference and index.
    ISBN 1-59003-016-8 (pbk.)
    1. Spirituality in art. 2. Creation (Literary, artistic, etc.) 3. Self-actualization
(Psychology) I. Title.
    N71 .A949 2002

Typeset in Sabon and Futura

Printed in Canada

TCP

09 08 07 06 05 04 03 02
  8 7 6 5 4 3 2 1

"My bed faces west," she told me. "I don't sleep at night, I look at the stars."

GEORGIA O'KEEFFE TO ARLENE RAVEN,
IN A *VILLAGE VOICE* INTERVIEW

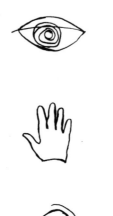

Contents

MEDITATIONS AND EXERCISES

      Italian Dog   97

10   Gardens for the Spirit   *98*
      Looking at the Moon   108

11   Opening the Heart toward
      Loving Kindness   *109*
         Jenny   124

12   Spirit Wheels   *127*

      List of Artists   *143*
      References and Further Reading   *145*

Acknowledgments

Special Thanks:

To my daughter, Nana Nicola Olivas, whose many conversations with me about the book were extremely helpful, and to my son-in-law, Jamie McEwen, whose thoughtful concern and good will were inspirational.

To Joanne Mattera, editor, and Jan Johnson, publisher, for their encouragement in believing this book possible and then making it so.

To my coach, Pamela Bloom, who spent admirable hours asking and questioning, coaching and coaxing.

To Harriet Lyons, my editor friend par excellence, who graciously read through the manuscript and gave me valuable advice.

To Berenice Fisher and Arlene Raven, whose detailed reviews of the manuscript were most helpful, as were their astute comments and suggestions.

To Arverna Adams, Joan Arbeiter, Hazel Belvo, Gayla Bjork, Phyllis Chesler, Linda Ferguson, Avital Greenberg, Suzanne Iasenza, Helene Kostre, Linda Marks, Susan McDonald, Dena Muller, Lynn Northrup, John O'Neill, Felecia Onofrietti, Ann Pachner, Paulette Pettorino, Flavia Rando, Phyllis Rosser, Margaret Sheffield and Elizabeth Stratton for their comments, contributions, and questions.

To Aaron Zimmerman of Manhattan Writers for his encouragement with my "writer's voice."

To Andrea Gilates and Phyllis Campbell of the Split Rock Arts Program at the University of Minnesota for their support and belief in my work while I taught many innovative and unusual programs there over the years.

To Ellen Donahue and Ronald Sosinski of Donahue/Sosinski Art, New York City where I exhibited my work from 1992 to 2000, for their support and encouragement.

To Charles Froelick of Froelick Gallery in Portland, Oregon, for his support.

To Roderic Crooks and Denise Lewis, my assistants, who have helped with so much detail.

And finally, to my many students over the years, who have taught me so much on the two-way street between teacher and participant.

With One Eye Open
(and One Eye Closed)

BRING me the sunset in a cup.

EMILY DICKINSON

Visual art, such as painting and sculpture, has its own kind of language. It reaches us in a way that words cannot, for words cannot be literally translated into visual form. Art is not only the pictorial description of something beautiful. As defined in this book, art is visual description in a language of shape, color, and form, presenting the viewer with a dialogue different from that found in words. It is a graphic manifestation of the way we think and feel.

By developing a visual sense and a visual form as a means to express that sense, and by viewing work that has a visual presence, we enter a more spacious dimension than words can offer. This visual dimension offers the possibility of wisdom as well as an expression of experience. Because it is a different kind of dimension from what we usually know through words, time spent with the visual can be a healing experience, a communication with spirit, and a way to make a connection to the divine.

This book is for those of you who want to expand and examine your own vision. It is for those of you who have never made art and are curious, for those of you who have stopped working for whatever reason, and even for those of you who are artists and want to rethink some ideas or try out the exercises and meditations. A major focus of this book is how artmaking is connected to our imagination and how our imagination is developed by meditation. The exercises and meditations are identified with the following icons:

hands-on exercises

visual exercises

meditations

The meditations and exercises in this book are ones I have used myself, because this book, by way of example, also follows my personal journey toward accessing my creative potential. I have shared them with students in workshops for twenty-five years, using the topics for self-exploration and for the making of art. As you will see, one is connected to the other. These ideas and methods were effective in inspiring me to make art, removing obstacles that stood in the way of my creative process, and bringing light to the sources that make up the components of who I am. When I have shared them in workshops, I have come away energized not only by the content, which one student described as having been "excavated from within my psyche," but by the lucid and strong images made into drawings, paintings, and sculptures by the participants.

My Sicilian grandfather used to say that he liked "to see the world with one eye opened and one eye closed." In true folktale manner, he left his proverb unexplained, but I like to think it was a metaphor to keep my right eye open to see my surroundings, and my left eye closed to the outside but looking inward at my intuition. Used together, the inner and the outer eyes give a fuller experience of the world and an opportunity to apply this perception to the creative process. I would be very happy if you approached this book in this manner. Think about my ideas, and explore yours in relation to them. Take time to experience the exercises and the meditations, skipping around if you choose. Bring this book with you to your worktable or studio, making it a companion to your artmaking process.

You may want to use the art you make from the exercises and meditations—the working drawings and collages, paintings, and in some cases sculpture—as material to be taken to the studio or not, to be translated into your other work or not, or to just to get you started.

My hope is that this book will give you insight into the expression of visual language and how it can be applied to your life as a catalyst for growth and change. My student Mary says that I represent a kind of spirit door to her, a door that opens and shines a light onto her mysteries on the other side of her everyday world. This is a good metaphor for what I want this book to be, a door that will open to that deep place in each of us. I hope to open that door and to help you find a spirit light within where you can view your inner self as if watching a film, see your personal images there, and find the place where your own spirit takes form.

part one

HAND and SPIRIT

1

the door opens

We all have to fight our obsessions and prejudices and try to keep our eyes open to new forms. I know I do, for one. It's very difficult to see something that's new, and not a repetition of something you've already seen and responded to. But if you can get into the right kind of receptive and appreciative—creative— way of seeing, then the whole world is full of new ideas and new possibilities. One of the things that modern art has done is to open people's eyes in that way.

HENRY MOORE

Materials for Letting Your Spirit Take Form

The artwork you make during our sessions together is your own personal information for getting you started or for reexamining your forms. However you work, whatever you come up with is fine. Make stick figures, be a child again, just let yourself be with your hand on the page openly expressing yourself. If you are just starting to work with art materials, you may find the following list of supplies helpful. Art supply stores carry all of these items.

Surround yourself with possibilities: an 11x14 drawing pad or larger (try to work with this size, as a smaller pad doesn't give you a chance to stretch out on the page). Choose an acid-free, all-purpose sketchpad instead of newsprint, which doesn't hold up.

Choose some or all of the following:

- Oil pastels
- Crayons
- A small box of charcoal sticks
- A box of watercolors
- 3B graphite pencils, (3B is a medium soft lead, you might

want to experiment with 2H (hard) or 6B (soft) as well

- 2 soft water color brushes, one very narrow, one wider
- A small set of acrylic paints, or tubes of the primary colors: red, yellow, blue, green, white and black
- A box of colored pencils
- A collection of magazine photos for collage; begin to collect them
- An assortment of colored papers
- Photocopies of family photos
- Scissors and glue (white glue preferred)

If you have more space and/or would like to add a third dimension to your artwork, here are some suggestions:

- Collect found objects that are small and manageable such as leaves, pebbles, and twigs (you can also make photocopies of these)
- Quick-drying clay
- Wood scraps or driftwood
- Papier-mâché
- Beads
- Interesting fabrics and thread
- Fabric glue
- Leather scraps

These supplies will give you the opportunity to work in different ways as your spirit guides you. If you have never used some of these materials, experiment with them. Make some marks on the page with the pencils, trying them out with some soft strokes and then some harder ones. Wet your brush (not too much water) and gently apply some of the watercolor to your paper, thickly so that the paint is opaque, and then thinly, so that it is translucent. With one of the oil pastels, press down hard on to the paper, giving it a burst of color. Now rub it with your finger and see how the color spreads out into a splash, deeper and lighter. Play with your materials. There is no one way to use any of them.

Cultivate two good habits: first, if you are able, keep your supplies out on a table always ready so that you can work easily, even a few minutes at a time. Even if you have a busy life or find it difficult to make time for your art, you can snatch moments from your life to make something as the need arises. Don't forget that looking at your work in progress is an important part of your process, so look as much as possible, thinking about it during the day, and your artwork will grow.

Second, save your artwork so that you can see your progress and grow to appreciate what you have done. Too often we discard something because we don't like it only to wonder later how it relates to what we're doing now, or intend to throw away something that on a second look is better than we thought.

About the Meditations We Will Do Together

Meditation is a very simple practice. It is often referred to as the cultivation of mindfulness, just noticing and being with what is. As you proceed to the guided meditations and other exercises in this book, begin by allowing yourself to relax.

I suggest you start each guided meditation in this way:

Sit in a chair with your feet flat on the floor, or cross-legged on a cushion, and become still and silent with yourself.

Fold your hands in your lap or rest them gently on your knees. Make yourself as comfortable as possible, as relaxed as possible, but stay clear-minded, alert, and aware, watching your thoughts.

Keep your spine straight, but don't force yourself into an

uncomfortable uprightness. Observe how your body fits into the chair or on the cushion, the sounds about you, and the rhythm of your breath. Notice yourself breathing in and out.

Observe your out breath. You might imagine your out breath as if it is riding the wings of a beautiful bird. The in breath is automatic, so just let it happen and focus on the out breath. Let every part of your body feel filled with light and released from tension.

Notice where the tension is and try to fill it with light and breath.

You can do the meditations and exercises in this book many times, and each time can bring you new, richer experiences and deeper insights. When doing them there is no need to push yourself beyond where you feel you can go. Stop where you feel it's right to stop, and begin to draw in that place. Just draw freely. What comes up in the drawing is where you are supposed to be. Each meditation will offer suggestions and ideas about materials, so don't worry now about what to draw.

All the meditations and exercises in this book are suggestions. If you find yourself going to images different from the ones that I suggest in a meditation, change them as you like. Follow your intuition. Each time you return to the meditations, you may find different images from the experience of the meditation, which is your personal story line about your life events and experiences. If you think of your intuition as subconscious logic—a kind of thinking in an intuitive way, a different way to make sense out of the world—it can expand rather than hold back these stories. Don't push yourself beyond where you feel comfortable with any of them.

If you are like some of my students who tell me that in their meditation they don't see anything, that "nothing" is all that they see, and that they get "nothing" out of it, I would ask you: What does nothing looks like? What color it is? How dark is it? What kind of shape does nothing have?

Put yourself into a picture with nothing. Frequently, this line of introspection can open up a place to start. It may help you to start drawing. Think about nothing. This idea always reminds me of mathematics. What is zero? Without zero we cannot have one. Without nothing we cannot have something.

Going to our inner vision and voice takes courage. At first the surprise of it can be a delight, but as you visit with your voice, say over the course of a week in a workshop, or as you work your way through this book, you can see parts of yourself that are difficult to acknowledge. Perhaps you will find anger or hurt that you may not have been aware of. Often you discover how you have built up barriers and made obstacles to encountering these feelings. You hear the voices of criticism or denial or find many veils and masks that prevent you from going within.

Finding your own vision in art can be a fearful thing even when you are drawn to it as a spiritual idea. Fear of fear makes life unpleasant because it makes the original fear even larger. We can either shut the door to this part of our self or help it to open and appreciate it. One way to open that door is to cultivate what is called the unconditional witness. There is a part of us that can observe who we are and all we do without judgment. This is so important in artmaking because it accepts us as we are and honors all the images and visions that come out of our imagination. Sogyal Rinpoche, the author of *The Tibetan Book of Living and Dying*, gives the meditation instruction of dividing your awareness into three parts—twenty-five percent on your breath, fifty percent on the space, and twenty-five percent on this unconditional witness. This technique takes a lot of daily practice. Seen as a fertile ground from which your inner world can arise, the unconditional witness can become your best friend and your ally in the process of both your daily life and your artmaking,

Learning (and teaching) about art from a place of spirit calls us to a challenge, a challenge to look at something so familiar, yet so remote. Still it is so clearly from within ourselves that we often neglect to honor it.

Let your self guide you.

Seven Gifts

Allow into your art space these seven gifts that come from working from your inner world:

The courage to sit and wait.

The curiosity to open closed doors and explore what is behind them.

The ability to listen to yourself.

An appreciation for the experience of all life.

A respect for the power of your imagination.

The compassion to try to embrace all things with unconditional acceptance.

And an awe for the path of knowing.

Let your self guide you.

THE FIG TREE

I was born in Brooklyn just before World War II, and my early childhood is now a mist in my memory. A mist of a beautiful rose garden with roses planted in a circle, a yearly fragrant burst of different reds, yellows, whites, and pinks. I have memories of peonies and of fruit trees on the lawn. There was a lush fig tree whose leaves and branches were cut off every fall—leaving only its naked trunk and its wounds, which were then sealed with tar. Its torso was subsequently wrapped like a mummy in tight bandages of burlap.

During much of my early life I felt like that fig tree, pruned and clipped and once in a while, even now, the bittersweet words of my father still circle in my head. He long ago explained that the fig tree was treated that way "for its own good," otherwise it would not survive the New York winter.

In the mist are familiar songs, such as "When Johnny Comes Marching Home" and "Don't Sit Under the Apple Tree with Anyone Else But Me," songs that I have only recently realized were from the tender side of the war. I was very little, but I can still hear the loving, animated voices of the Italian-American adults and their fear and panic, frightened for their adopted country, and worried for those left on the "other side." I can still remember their concern escalating with every new report and their confusion at the inexplicable, unspeakable brutality and pain.

I can also bring back to mind the feelings of the darkly lit church in our parish, with its flickering votive candlelight which drew large, formidable shadows on the walls during the long hours of Sunday Mass when I had to sit very still. And as I think back now, I can hear the soft murmurs of old women caught up in fervent prayer.

2

Personal Journeys

I grew up pretty much as everybody else grows up and one day seven years ago found myself saying to myself—I can't live where I want to—I can't go where I want to—I can't do what I want to—I can't even say what I want to. School and things that painters have taught me even keep me from painting as I want to. I decided I was a very stupid fool not to at least paint as I wanted to and say what I wanted to when I painted as that seemed to be the only thing I could do that didn't concern anybody but myself— that was nobody's business but my own.

GEORGIA O'KEEFFE

I have always felt a special connection to the artist Georgia O'Keeffe. I first looked at her lush flower paintings in an exhibition at the Whitney Museum in the early 1970s. Her paintings made me feel as if I had entered them, as if I had put myself in the middle of each canvas and become a person/flower experiencing the world. The power of these works, the fact that Georgia O'Keeffe was able to find essential images in flowers and paint them onto canvas, helped give me permission to pursue my own vision. This is not easy. Most people are unable to pursue their own vision by themselves.

The intense need for my own personal journey in art has led me from painting on canvas and making clay figures of the body to becoming a sculptor in wood. For many years now I have been painting gold- and silver-leafed sculptures and assembled pieces of carved wood. I also make collages and drawings. My art has been referred to as "spiritually infused" because it is involved with myth and ritual and because of its concern both with the magical qualities and healing properties inherent in the process and the finished work of art.

I now believe that anyone can make art. In my thirty-five years of teaching, I have always found this to be true. I didn't always feel that way. I never thought that I could make art when I was a child.

I loved to make things, but I never thought of myself as an artist. Even though I knew somehow that art was natural to everyone, I couldn't make the leap necessary to do it. Making art was for artists. I didn't think I had ability because representational art—both that of Michelangelo and commercial art out of magazines—was what everybody in my southern Italian family praised and admired. My desire to pursue art was great, but my ability to do it was held back by other people's definitions of what I should be able to put on the page. I eagerly painted by numbers, made leather-craft wallets, and assembled crepe paper flowers, but to create from an empty space, a blank canvas or a bare wood stump, was not even considered, let alone encouraged.

I did have some early glimpses about the nature of art. The process of becoming an artist began in my grandfather's garden in the Dyker Heights section of Brooklyn where I grew up. When I think about the things that have formed my sense of self as an artist, I always return to those lessons from the garden. The garden heightened my sense of observation, awakened my curiosity, and made me comfortable with solitude. It opened my eyes to an appreciation of colors and shapes, and brought me wonder at its different cycles.

Because there were no children my age in my neighborhood, I was often left alone in the garden to play by myself. I would watch the flowers and leaves grow and die. My child self would not know that they would return. Their return brought awe and disbelief. It is still so vivid in my mind: the explosion of colors in the spring, the change of colors in the fall. The brilliance of the sun, the softness of the moon, the shadows cast by the trees. The rhythm and patterns of spacing and thinning, shaping and pruning, of watching things change, of seeing birds and plants mature and die. My grandfather and his gardener worked there with such love and caring.

I used to lie on the grass under the flowers, pressing my body into the damp earth as I watched the daily comings and goings of garden life. There were fragrant lilies of the valley lining the side of the garage. An abandoned doghouse with its musty smell brought to life the image of lost dogs and children. There was a victory garden with lettuce, (*lattuga* my father would say,) zucchini, and string beans. A neighbor's garden was behind a vine-covered fence where I could watch huge summer squashes with their exotic southern Italian names—zucchini, *cocozz'*, *cuccuzelle*. A neat row of proud wild cherry trees separated the property. As I watched the loving-ness and the passion of my grandfather and his gardener, I learned from him how to bring that same kind of attention to my art.

Another important lesson about the nature of art took place when I was six years old. As part of a class trip I saw the mummies at the Brooklyn Museum. The teacher was chattering on about the life of the mummies and I remember wishing she would be quiet, because I was experiencing a light in them and the sound of her voice distracted me. An inexplicable radiance was permeating everything. In fact, everything in my sight was permeated with light emanating from the inside of the mummy cases. It was a light and a magic I had never experienced before in anything else except when lying on the grass on the damp earth in my grandfather's garden. All I wanted was to be in that light and to learn about that light and live in that light. Something inexplicable opened to me. It had all seemed very strange but special, and I kept it to myself, not daring to share it with anyone.

The first time that I heard it was possible for me to become an artist was twelve years later when I was interviewed for a class in fashion design taught by Christine Block, a teacher at Finch College in New York City. She told me emphatically, "If you can write your own name, you can learn to draw." News to me, I thought, but I guess I will try it. Timidly I signed up for her class. During the semester I found that my hand could develop a memory for information about vision just as it had learned to make letters. I have never turned back.

After graduating from Finch, I became a costume designer for the theater in New York City. Although I loved what I was doing and had fun with it, I began to look for something more artistically challenging. Gradually, I thought that maybe art was what I was looking for. I experimented with canvas and paints. My first painting tried to capture the light from the lampost across the street from where I lived. I made an almost life-sized painting of the black metal streetlight head, and then I tried to paint the light that radiated from within it. At the time no one liked it. I am not sure whether even I liked it, because it was odd looking, not pleasant to look at.

I know now that I wasn't looking for a pretty picture. What I was looking for was a way to describe radiance and to put it into paint, a way to make a relationship between this radiance and the spiritual aspect of artmaking. I was obsessed with painting those rays from that streetlight. I spent hours on them. The result was not that interesting, but it was a start. How odd it is to look back at that first painting from where I am now many years later, as an artist who uses an abundance of gold leaf in her sculpture. It is curious that even then, when I was twenty years old, I was trying to do with paints what I do now. That part is the same. It runs through all of my artwork: a desire to express the radiance. But at that time it was all buried under the surface of myself.

That first painting inspired me, and I signed up for some classes at the Art Students League in New York City. As I made a head, body, or figure, I would realize that over and over again particular forms and marks would surface—long lines across the page, obsessive circles, odd angular shapes. But art school convention held that unskilled and unformed vestiges had no honorable place. Teachers told me to erase them. I learned to tell myself, "that's not right. I have to change the shape." I would erase this form and cover it over with something that was more acceptable to the teacher and to the conventions I was learning.

In art school, the primary idea was

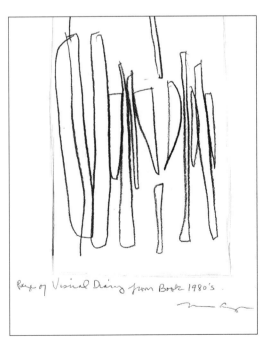

Page of Visual Diary from Book 1980's.

to learn how to draw and paint from the model. In this way you learned how to see. Learning how to see meant training your eyes so that they could discern and develop a sensitivity to what was in front of you. Most of us never focus our eyes on what is in front of us. In my painting and sculpture classes, I would look and look day after day for hours at a time, trying to capture what was in front of me. The painting instructor, Edwin Dickinson, wanted us to paint a section of the model, a shoulder say, or a breast. We weren't permitted to paint the head since he felt that we brought too many "preconceived notions" to the head. We were to look at our little section as if it was the first time we had ever seen it. And in truth, it was the one and only time that particular model would be exactly like that, never before, never again. Looking so hard and so long brought out aspects of the images very different from those shapes and forms that I had thought made up a shoulder or a knee. I saw a fuller, clearer image. I looked at things with a much clearer eye and was able to translate them onto paper or canvas, or into clay.

This was important training for which I have great respect. But after art school I was lost. I was in this new role of artist, and it didn't fit well. I had learned enough rules, but I would stare for hours at the log to be carved or the paper to be marked and ask myself over and over, what can I make? What was truly mine now that I had an opportunity to envision it? Where were those shapes and forms that belonged to me, that were yearning to come out? How could I find them? I would sit day after day looking, waiting, drawing, and thinking.

Gradually, in the silence, a kind of door would open for me in my mind. How can I describe this for you? When I am in that space, I often think: What does it sound like, look like, this same space—also described in meditation—which is between thoughts, a place between thought and thought? Sometimes it comes up in an image with the form of myself standing at the edge of a high stone cliff looking out over to the edge of the stone cliff next to it. Between the two cliffs is a chasm, narrow yet endlessly deep. This narrow place functions as an ellipsis does in a sentence, as a kind of pause between one thought and the next. In that pause dwell my personal shapes and forms that inspire me to grapple with the questions that hover around essence.

I discovered this space by myself, but the door was barely opened. There was a constant battle between what I thought was the right thing to put down on the paper and what my hand wanted to say. Eventually, I began to understand what had happened. It was the difference between working from a formula and from my own heart. Skill is important but without heart, art is lifeless. It's like one of those oranges that is lovely and beautiful on the outside, but has nothing inside—no sweet fruit, no juice. No spirit to take form.

Opening the Door to Your Creative Space Within

This meditation will guide you to your creative space and help you become familiar with how it functions. This is your "inner studio." Use this meditation to visit it as often as you like.

Imagine a comfortable, cozy room.

Visualize your body as pure light that becomes the room and everything in it.

Spend a few minutes becoming familiar with how that feels, seeing yourself as luminous light with its warm lovely rays all around you, all of those beautiful rays filling the room from within you, like a rainbow coming to you and from within you.

Now with your mind's eye, notice the walls in your room, the height of the room, and the shape of the room.

Put yourself, as you know yourself, as you are now, into this room.

What are you wearing?

Find a place for yourself in the room.

Do you recognize this room as a space you have known, or is it new for you? It is a comfortable place for you to express your creative self, to make your artwork.

Be comfortable and relaxed in this room.

Just be there, relaxed, calm,

Enjoy what is there, what is familiar to you.

Spend some time there getting more information about it for yourself. Imagine yourself moving around in this room and see more of its "nature," its presence, and its character.

Now put windows and doors in your room, if you haven't already. See where you place them in the room. See what kinds of windows they are.

Now open them up. Let the open doors and windows bring something new and unexpected, or ancient and forgotten, into the room. What comes in? Who comes in?

Now ask why it has come and what it wants from you and how it is connected to your creative desire. Be it person or object, give it a voice. Let it tell you what it wants from you and why.

Now ask it to help you with your artwork and to become a companion to your artmaking process.

Make a note of yourself as pure light, and notice how you fill your room with radiance.

In your mind's eye place around you all of the things you need to make art—crayons, pencils, paints, photos, whatever you need to begin this process for you.

This room is your "inner studio."

Spend some time and get acquainted with it.

Draw your room with its walls, windows and doors, and the things for your artwork in it.

Drawing Your Inner Studio

I frequently envision an inner space that was the roof garden of a loft in which I once lived. It had a beautiful corner trellis of climbing red roses. When the sun came there, I used to stand with my beloved white German Shepherd and feel pleasure at being alive. In my visions I often put my workspace there.

Another place that I imagine is *The Spirit House of the Mother*, a large sculpture that I made in 1994. It is a sanctuary—ten feet by seven feet by six feet, carved from Douglass fir logs—that can be entered by an open entrance. Its outer surface has thirty-two carved wood panels with gold leaf, but its interior is magenta and pearlescent pink with deep maroon spirals. It is a place to honor the Divine Feminine, the nurturing mother in myself and in all of us.

Using broad or narrow marks, or both together, draw the outline of an imaginary space on an 11"x14" piece of paper. This will be your inner studio. This studio can be whatever shape comes to mind, such as a circle or triangle. It doesn't have to be at all realistic, since it is a room for your spirit.

Within your outline, find a special place where you will be able to work. Put your worktable there. It can be your kitchen table, an easel, a workbench, or whatever you envision. Select the spot where you will be sitting, and mark it with a shape and a color.

Now take colored paper and choose colors that feel right and make shapes out of them, shapes to represent the spirit part of your studio. Rip or cut three or four shapes carefully. Glue them into your inner studio. This collage will represent the spirit forms in your studio.

Something to remember: If you can't find images in your mind's eye, make them up. You are trying to have your spirit take form, and sometimes making it up—tapping into your unconscious—is the best way to uncover her.

THE FABRIC

The fabric has been in a cedar trunk for thirty-five years. I remember when I bought it. I don't exactly remember the circumstances, but I remember its elegance and its feel. I have always thought that the color, a vibrant Navajo turquoise, was the wrong color for me, for my complexion, but I wanted it anyway. Maybe just to look at it and touch it was enough then. Its thick, double-layered satin is the kind of surface, woven with fine silk threads, that almost reflects your image when you look into it. I have saved and saved it. I have always thought I would use it with some other fabric and make a jacket for an opening of one of my shows—a special exhibition, a museum retrospective, say. I would wear this satin, made into a jacket with black velvet sleeves and collar. But there it sits waiting in the trunk.

This fabric, so sumptuous to touch, brings all kinds of sensory pleasure to me. It's expansive and open and it extends itself. It was the opposite of my childhood in which everything was all so planned, plotted, and expected. Narrow like a camera's eye, more and more focused on the "only way," "the right way," the rules and regulations of every moment of the day. This fabric, with its fine weave and in-your face-elegance, represents everything my childhood could not be. It represents abandon, loss of control, center stage, spotlights, and accomplishment—the accomplishment of a well-behaved girl child who struggled and succeeded in becoming her own woman.

3

Visual Diaries

To us art is an adventure into an unknown world which can be explored only by those who are willing to take risks.

ADOLPH GOTTLIEB AND MARK ROTHKO

It was a very exciting time in the 1970s. I was discovering a place of empowerment inside myself. I was so grateful to be alive because I could be involved in feminism, which for me meant exploring everything. Nothing was out of reach. The impact of feminism on many women artists inspired a women's cultural movement. Being part of a consciousness-raising group, I discussed, discovered, examined everything from the very essence of my birth to my life as a woman, to the forms, colors, and shapes that I put into my art. I asked myself, what was male? What was female? Could the divine be gendered female? What would that be like? Were there unique female images? What did they look like? How were they relevant? Some of us examined women's traditional ways of working, such as quilting, rug braiding, weaving, which until then had been considered lesser forms of art. We considered them as important as paintings and sculptures.

The idea that "the personal is political" was a revelation. I began to incorporate this idea into my life and my art. It was a whole new way of thinking for me. Before then, the personal was belittled, as something that only women were engaged in and, therefore, not important. My everyday experience developed a relevance that I no longer ignored or dismissed but included in relationship to my art-work.

At this time, as an experiment, I began drawing during these consciousness-raising⁺ sessions, to try to record visually what was being said. It was an unsuccessful project because the conversations could not be translated visually. However, I found that by doing original "primitive" drawings, forms belonging only to me would surface. In fact, I noticed that the same forms—those long lines, circles, and angular shapes similar to the kind of images that I had been taught to erase in art school—kept returning. Even then I found myself erasing them. But I came to treasure them, realizing they had emotional import as an expression in shapes and colors of the *emotional* dialogue taking place. A new presence beyond words kept emerging through these forms. When I finally allowed them to come through completely, my work began to flower. Eventually, I accepted my obsession with these lines and shapes as natural and normal. Later, I wondered if the experience of drawing during a discussion might be as liberating and stimulating for others as it was for me.

In 1979, I co-founded a feminist art school, The New York Feminist Art Institute (NYFAI) with Miriam Schapiro, Carol Stronghilos, Irene Peslikis, Lucille Lessane, and Selina Whitefeather. It was our intent to examine issues relating to gender, self, and identity. For my first workshop there, I devised a way to share my experience in a class called "Consciousness-Raising, Visual Diaries, Artmaking." As we did consciousness-raising that first year in a classroom setting, we chose a topic, and each woman drew in a blank

---

⁺Consciousness-raising is a method of discussion used by many women in the 1970s to understand how their lives were shaped. We would sit in a circle and talk about a particular topic, always using ourselves as the subject to describe it. We honored the use of the word "I." Before this wave of feminism, women especially used "we" or "one" to discuss themselves and others. Using "I" was considered impolite and self-important, which we were never to permit ourselves to be. This was the first time in my life that I remember saying, "I did this. I felt this. I thought this," and others would listen to me. We listened to each other without interrupting or trying to fix each other.

book while the others spoke in turn, making a visual record of what was said. The drawings that came out of the workshop confirmed what I had found, that the shapes and forms unique to each of the participants were repeatedly found in her work.

One of the rules of the class was that each participant was to treat her drawings as if they were personal diary entries of her inner life, not for publication or display. As the women became startled with the freshness and newness of their visual pieces, I reminded them that these images hadn't come from another world to visit them. Rather they were part of the interior landscape with which the women lived all the time and had not noticed, or just barely noticed, or had erased as I had done.

It was thrilling to be part of their discovery. I watched women change their processes, many returning to art after years of being stuck. Others shifted gears and made more authentic images. We drew and made collages, built up pages in our books, and made substantial and powerful diaries. We showed only sections of them if we chose to in exhibitions at NYFAI, tying off the other pages with ribbon or clipping them together to keep private what was not ready to be revealed. In those books were new visions, ideas, ways of seeing—shadows from the past.

Making Your Visual Diary

Making a visual diary will help you uncover the forms that are yours. If you can incorporate diary making into your daily life, you and your art will have an ongoing relationship. (Making a diary is also a good way to prepare for the meditations in this book.) Joan Arbeiter, one of the first participants in my visual diaries workshop at NYFAI, writes that her visual diaries were made from the "stuff of my ordinary daily life. Mundane notions such as shopping lists, appointments, and phone numbers were used along with philosophical commentary, overheard bits of dialogue, and other sayings that came my way. These words were often grouped into shapes that 'read' as

Page of Visual Diary from Book 1980's

Page of Visual Diary from Book 1980's

Page of Visual Diary from Book. 1980's.

images along with doodles, designs, and sketches. It was in fact soon after the workshop that I began to integrate these ideas into my own large format paintings and drawings."

Buy a bound blank book. (Bound books are best because you are less likely to tear out the pages.)

Keep this book with you as much as possible.

Keep it open at home with your crayons and pencils next to it.

But they don't lie flat when open.

Bring it with you when you travel or have a separate one in your pocket or purse to take with you.

Try not to write in your book at first, so that you can train yourself to work only visually instead of relying on more familiar verbal expression.

Store it as you would a personal diary. If you think of it as a for-your-eyes-only volume, you will give yourself more freedom.

Don't erase what you make. If you don't like it, turn the page and make a new drawing.

Just begin to work on the new page and see where it takes you.

Try not to think about or judge what you are making.

Begin to keep a record of your activities for a day and then the next and so on, but be gentle with yourself—no need to feel bad, work when you can.

Draw your life day to day.

If you miss a day (or a week), just continue when you are able.

Draw, collage, or paint in it when you are inclined to.

Be free and open. Be spontaneous.

Make marks in it.

Paint masks in it.

Draw cubes and squares in it.

Make a special code for yourself in it.

Or a secret language in it.

Express onto the page whatever comes up.

Do it as automatically as you can, without thinking or planning.

Especially try to record your experiences, keeping in mind that the translation of visual information is not the same as words.

Draw what you feel, what you think, what you see.

Draw what you would like to know.

Draw your friends ~~~~~~ ~ily, not just what they look like, but perhaps symbols ~~~~~~~~~~ vou feel.

Improvise.

Draw the thir

Put a leaf ir

Draw a b

Trace y

Trace

Dra

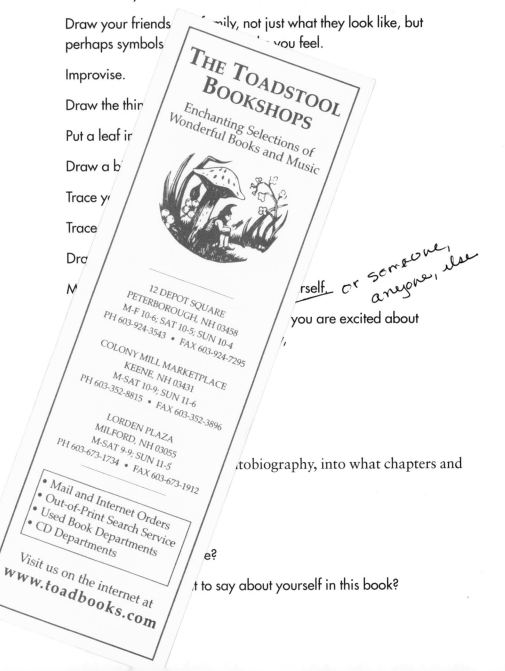

M   rself. or someone, anyone, else

                                     you are excited about

                            .tobiography, into what chapters and

                      e?

                 t to say about yourself in this book?

What would you like to portray?

How would you use color and shape for this?

Describe an ordinary day in your life.

Lynn Northrup, a curious beginner, from the early NYFAI Visual Diaries workshop writes, "I loved working with colored markers and crayons. With no specific intent in mind, I could choose whatever color I wanted and make any design or mark I wanted to on the page in front of me. There was to be no judgment from others on what I did, only a chance to share my doodlings if I wished. I loved using bright colors, making lines and all different shapes on the blank pages while I listened and spoke in my turn."

Consider forming a drawing group in which you and other participants can get together and talk about your lives, even do consciousness-raising if you like and draw in your books as others speak. Whether you meet once a week or once a month, put aside every forth meeting time to discuss your visual diary with the rest of the group. Try to describe the essence of the experience, using paint, colored pencils, crayons, pencils or a collage of magazine photos.

Linda Ferguson, a participant in my "Visual Diaries/Artist's Books" workshop writes that when she runs into road blocks in her studio, (in other words gets stuck), she remembers my suggestion to "make it up," "which was like a revelation! Those three words are a tape that still plays in my mind when I am up against a wall. They are one of the gems I carry with me because they break through my illusionary blocks and return me to possibility again, accompanied by an enormous emotional relief leaving a tremendous sense of freedom and control and affording me the belief that I can do it."

THE SOUND OF THE MALLET

Today was a good day to carve, to take that chisel and the mallet in hand and go into the wood, to make the inverted leaf forms that I have been trying to get to for days. I love to hear the rhythm of the mallet hitting the chisel and to see the shape of the cut as the chisel breaks through. It's a very musical rhythm, tapping, tapping, hitting into the forms, giving them a presence and a life. Tap, tap, tap, whap, whap. I have been doing it for so long I have taken for granted its meaning and its place in my life. It took the writing of this book, when I carved less often, to show me what is missing when I don't do it. Carving with its daily ritual, gives a defined form to my life, a kind of vision that is so central to my experience of self.

Is it that every day I see myself a little closer to giving a shape to something out of the wood? Is it the daily routine of being there, doing the same repetitive motion over and over, one that fills up my morning hours that I am attached to? Day after day, every morning except when I can't because I am going to the dentist or have some other appointment, I am there, straight from my dreams, right out from their source. I wonder how important is the sound of the mallet, is the feeling of the warm dreams still flashing in my mind playing across the landscape behind my eyes? I often use my hand, my fingertips, to see what I am doing, only later using my eyes. It's that feeling sense, that sense of self inside of the wood that is important, that makes the work come alive. If it doesn't come alive, then it doesn't have the ability to speak its language. It remains dead, a dead piece of wood without history or memory of its life, a piece of lumber. No reaching, no calling, no voice.

Sometimes in a desperate attempt to find its life, I call out to it, struggle to ask it to speak to me, demand that it respond. Sometimes it does, leading me to the next stroke and the next.

Sometimes, when it comes to that, I have threatened it, demanded that it speak, accused it of being uncaring and silent in the face of my pleas, pleading with it to open up and show me its heart, a heart which refuses to open up and let me in. It's really true that wood does have a heart, and a memory, and a history. It's just hard for wood to share them with a human, especially when it has been cut and removed from its roots and is being asked to perform.

4

Beginner's Mind

In the beginner's mind there are many possibilities, but in the expert's there are few.

SHUNRYU SUZUKI, *ZEN MIND, BEGINNER'S MIND*

My first teaching job was working with the blind. I had never taught art before and was eager to learn. Most of the participants worked in clay, though some hammered metal and some made mosaic bowls. Their artwork was not what I was used to. They pressed and pulled the clay using hands and fingertips to affect the shapes. Figures evolved very differently from how I, a sighted person, would have made them. And yet they were strong and powerful and had their own particular presence in which eyes and hands were very prominent. Participants in the classes were able to see their work by touching it. With a caress, their fingertips had eyes and were given sight in ways that I had never before imagined. Approaching my sculpture in this new way, I used my fingertips to see what I was doing and later, my eyes.

According to the ideas of Zen Buddhism, my mind became in touch with Zen mind or beginner's mind. As Zen master Richard Baker, in his introduction to *Zen Mind, Beginner's Mind*, describes, "The Zen of calligraphy is to write in the most straightforward, simple way as if you were a beginner, not trying to make something skillful or beautiful but simply writing with full attention" (Baker, p. 14). Approaching artmaking with this intention of seeing each time as if for the first time with fresh new eyes is like having a great jewel in our midst. Baker goes on: "the innocence of the first inquiry. . . . The mind of the beginner is empty, free of the habits of the expert, ready to accept, to doubt, and open to all of the possibilities" (Baker, p. 13). I would say using the idea of artmaking in this context, those forms, which are yours, surface when you are at work. There become so many possibilities in the desire to create.

The desire to create is natural in all of us. Watch a child. Erik Erikson points out in *Childhood and Society* that children's work is actually their play. Children play with sounds as they begin to speak. They look and touch the things in their life to begin to place them in an order, to make visual sense of them. They sort flowers and leaves in their environments to order them; they move their food around in a creative way.

My daughter, Nana Nicola, used to play in my studio when she was about two years old. As I carved the logs that would become my sculpture, she would take up each wood chip that she liked, glue it onto a page, and make her own artwork. She did not know exactly what she was going to make, but she had enough of a sense of it that if I picked up a wood chip and put it on her paper she would demand that it be removed. Somewhere she knew what she wanted to do. It had to be exact and just right for her, and she knew when the picture was finished. She could describe it in great detail—this was a house, that was a family member, they were going out or in—in a way that I couldn't see myself. I was always surprised at the clarity and determination of her vision.

I remember Nana's childhood friend Jason, a frequent guest at sleepovers. At breakfast on the mornings when he visited, he would pile cereal in little sections, stacking them up on different sides of the bowl, eating only the shapes that he liked and moving aside the others, defending his choices with great determination. Even though Jason may not have known what the result would be, he knew exactly where each thing should go. Only when he finished sorting things out could he begin to eat, satisfied that his cereal story for that morning was complete.

As Erickson found in his research, sorting, stacking, and organizing are natural for children. It's play. And play for them is really a learning experience. They integrate inner dilemmas, teach themselves speech, orient themselves to new visual and aural patterns, all through play. This is the way children learn how to be in the world. As we become older and more involved in formal education, we lose our connection to this way of being, and with it go the excitement, enthusiasm, and freshness of childhood. When you are an artist, you can again see the world with the eyes of the child—with the "beginner's eyes" and "beginner's mind."

Using Your Eyes in a New Way

One way to stimulate "beginner's mind" in yourself is to look around. Notice everything. Touch it too, if you can. Follow each object with your body as well as your eyes to see these things. Notice the contours and surfaces of the objects that you see. Look for positive and negative spaces. Try to really see everything around you, people, trees, animals, plants, and as you look, feel how your body responds, how things shift in you.

Sculptor Auguste Rodin described in his book, *Art,* how he carved his figures by imagining that he was inside of them pushing out. Looking at Rodin's sculpture *The Thinker*, I can feel that power, as if the artist is living inside of and knows intimately this figure that he has made.

> Look at art. For instance, Pablo Picasso painted the many women in his life, each with her distinct personality, by using different forms and colors to portray each one. Compare his work to the paintings of Willem de Kooning, whose women, painted with broad strokes on the canvas, are fiery and fierce, and to the elegant and formal portraits of John Singer Sargent. Take a look at the sculptures of Louise Bourgeois, whose powerful sculptures in metal, wood, stone, or cloth are brought to life from the memory of her childhood and her dreams, or at

the works of Faith Ringgold, who calls on memories and stories to make her quilts and soft sculptures.

Study the sculptures of Louise Nevelson, who gathered segments and sections of furniture and other found wood objects and assembled them into large relief collages, which she painted with graphite to be a silvery gray. Looking at them, I see a window into how my mind divides into little sections or compartments, thoughts repeated over and over, changing slightly each time.

Georgia O'Keeffe, Barbara Hepworth, Henri Matisse, Paul Klee—so many artists, so many different visions. You can go to the twelfth century and find the vibrant illuminations of Hildegard of Bingen depicting her belief that all of creation is a symphony of joy and jubilation, or to the thirteenth century Florentine, Giotto, whose luminescent paintings of angels and other celestial figures may make you feel that you have entered another world.

Find your favorites and get to know them.

Become friends not only with European art but with art that comes from other cultures, such as that of Native Americans, Chinese, Africans, and Tibetans. Cultures that are different from ours give us different eyes—another kind of "beginner's eye"—because we are often looking at something in their art that we have never quite seen before. Consider African power figures from the Congo. Carved in wood and embedded with nails, iron blades, cloth, tacks, and glass, they are sacred protective figures. Consider the sculptures from the Dogon in West Central Africa, sculptures so essential to a village that to remove them was to take away the souls of the ancestors, according to Susan Vogel and Francine N'Diaye, authors of *African Masterpieces*. For a general overview of art history, you might refer to the two volumes of *Art History* by Marilyn Stokstad (see References and Further Reading).

Contemporary American and European artists of the last two centuries learned from the artists of these other cultures. Jackson Pollock made an intense study of Native American art, especially Navajo sand paintings. The influence of Mexican art on the sculpture of Henry Moore was significant for him, as was the folk art of Catalonia and Africa on the works of Picasso. Henri Matisse was deeply influenced by the decorative art of Algeria and Morocco, multimedia artist Meret Oppenheim with prehistoric art as seen in *Self-Portrait since 60,000 BC to X*, Pierre Bonnard by Persian paintings, Constantin Brancusi by folk art from his native Romania. The list continues to the contemporary German sculptor Joseph Beuys's engagement with Siberian art and shamans, and the English artist Anish Kapoor's work with the influence of the Indian art of his ancestors.

Looking at the ancient is also a powerful way to gain access to new ways of looking. I spent years studying the meaning of the hieroglyphics in the *Egyptian Book of the Dead*, drawing them and interpreting their pictorial meaning. In the April 3, 2001 edition of the *New York Times*, it was reported that German installation artist and painter Anselm Keifer is using the Sefer Hekhaloth, the ancient Jewish mystical tracts that describe the search for God at the center of the seven heavenly palaces, as inspiration. "The Hekhaloth is the spiritual journey toward perfect cognition," he said.

Sometimes breaking our perceptions of familiar objects brings us back to "beginner's mind." What if we ask: Why do painters use brushes? How are brushes made? Why not use a hand or a foot? Or a twig? (Some artists do.) Why has it been traditional to paint on a rectangle, and for how long? Why use canvas or oils, or stone, or wood, or plastic, or video?

Looking at Art

My friend Pamela, a musician and writer, asked me how she should look at a work of art. "You are writing this book about art," she said. "Will you be telling people like me how to look at a painting or sculpture? How would I begin?"

Select a painting or sculpture to look at, ideally one in the contemplative quiet of a museum. Begin by noticing your first impression the moment you look at it, and by continuing to be aware of your impressions as you draw closer to it: from twenty feet, from ten feet, and then close up. Put your body directly in front of it. Feel it with your eyes. "A picture lives by companionship, expanding and quickening in the eyes of the sensitive observer," wrote the painter Mark Rothko (Rothko, p. 565). Approach it like a new acquaintance. What is it that attracts you? Or repels you? To look at a work of art is to pay attention to what is there even if you don't like it. What is there? Try listing in your mind what you see. Let your eyes look in the center first and then move around it. Notice the colors and shapes, the forms from left to right, say, or top to bottom. What is the surface like? Is it reflective? Opaque? Rough? Smooth? Does it draw you into it? How do you feel about it? In other words, how does it speak to you? What do you feel that the artist is trying to say in it? You might want to write down what you see. I know that it's not translatable into words, but just try. It will bring you insight.

Bring your "beginner's mind" forward to think about the object in a picture or sculpture. Think about how and where the object is placed. You cannot have an object without its surroundings. Ask yourself: What is empty space? A sculpture cannot exist without the space around it, so it is the empty form around that gives ground to the full form.

Is your idea of an empty space a blank wall? Is it an empty room? Is it a landscape like a field? One of the things that artists agonize about is how the space changes when even a small section of the space is altered, such as a red turning into a pink in a corner, for example. Once the least little part of the surface changes, the whole picture shifts. Making a painting or a sculpture is a dynamic, moment-by-moment activity, one decision influencing every decision that comes after it. The act of looking at a work of art has some of that same energy, depending on whether you look from left to right or top to bottom of center to edges.

Another question you don't have to answer, but that you should think about, is: What language is the artwork trying to express? If you don't like the particular work, what would it need in order for you to like it? Why don't you like it? What must a visual experience, a work of art, have in order to mean something to you? For years, my father would look at my abstract artwork and ask, "Why don't you make something that looks like something?" While I did know what he meant, I would always think, "What does *something* really look like?"

Phyllis Rosser, who has been a participant in several of my workshops, has reminded me that I told her everybody has her or his own personal mark, and that this can especially be seen in Jackson Pollock's paintings. "This was a breakthrough for me in understanding Pollock's art," she says. "Before that it just looked like a jumble of lines, chaotic and messy."

Developing Your Visual Memory

This exercise will help you to learn to "see" and may change the way you think about things as well as the way you draw them. It's a bit different than the other exercises, a kind of fundamental, basic one. See if you can make "looking" part of your everyday life.

> Go into a familiar room and make yourself comfortable. Take a few minutes to look carefully around. As you do, memorize what is there. For example, see a favorite chair in the center of the room, see the curtains with the light coming through the windows, see a table.
>
> Let your eyes memorize all of these things that you see.

Now close your eyes and visualize in your mind's eye this room.

Recreate the visual image of this room with your eyes closed.

Open your eyes and look around and note again very carefully what is there.

Now take a drawing pad, oil pastels, pencils, and whatever else you like and go into another room.

Draw your room from memory.

Capture the things in it that you remember from your looking.

When your drawing is finished, compare what you drew from memory with your actual room. Notice the differences between what's there and what you drew. But remember, this is an exercise in developing your visual memory; it is not an easy one and not a demand for perfection.

Train yourself to use your eyes in a new way.

You can practice this anywhere even with out a drawing pad by deeply concentrating on what you see. When cooking, walking down the block, sitting at a meeting, or going out for the evening, use your eyes in a new way. Focus and look at everything with fresh eyes.

The Experience of Being Born

Before my daughter was born, a sculptor friend gave me a large log from a maple tree that had been felled by a hurricane. It was massive, three feet wide at the trunk, and as it sat in my studio, I almost felt that it was waiting for me to describe Nana's birth. In 1967, after her birth, I made the maple log into a carving, *Birth Piece*, freezing the moment in time when she entered the world. This sculpture uses the rich grain of the maple to simulate the energy of her birth, and the crotch of the wood for the moment of her entrance, the crowning. The meditation that follows will enhance your beginner's mind.

This is a meditation about your own birth.

Go to the base of your spine and bring your light there.

Spend a moment and imagine yourself as you are now, as if you are taking a snapshot of yourself.

Go deeper and deeper with your mind into your unconscious.

See this snapshot and spend a moment with it.

Now in your mind, gradually take yourself back, back in time.

Become smaller and smaller and younger and younger, until you see yourself no longer in this body and luminous with white light. You are now clear luminous light, a pure energy being suspended in the universe.

Feel yourself as this pure energy being.

What is it like for you? What does it feel like? What do you look like as a pure energy being? What color and shape are you? How big are you?

Spend some time sensing this.

Now watch yourself being drawn into your mother's body, becoming the smallest little being receiving food and nurturance from this pocket of protection in her body.

Give yourself a moment to savor this experience.

Now look around at your surroundings.

What kind of a place is your mother's womb?

Are you warm and comfortable?

Is it harsh or cold?

Are you cramped?

Is it confusing?

Are you safe?

Do you feel protected and warm?

Are you hungry?

Do you have enough to eat?

Are you getting what you want and need?

Do you feel wanted?

Do you feel wanted and loved?

What colors and shapes do you see?

What shape are you?

What shapes surround you?

How do you fit into your surroundings?

Are you upside down? Do you feel as if you are floating?

Now watch yourself growing larger and larger.

Know that you are about to leave this protected space and become a separate being.

Feel yourself beginning to move away from your mother, until you are being gradually pushed through the birth canal.

What does it feel like as you pass through that narrow corridor of muscle and flesh?

What is your body like there?

You are moving through a dark tunnel.

Do you want this?

Are you fearful?

Can you breathe?

What is happening to you?

How do you feel?

Do you feel lonely?

Anxious?

Are you glad to be separate?

See yourself gradually moving farther and farther until you are at the moment of your birth.

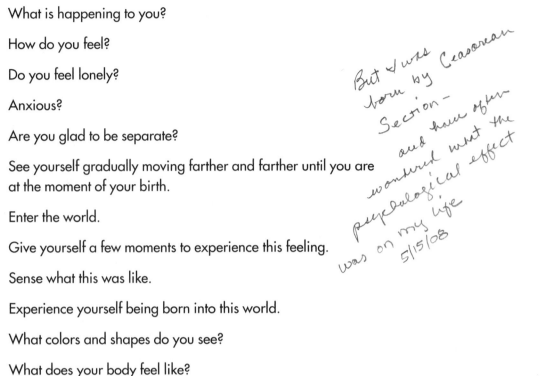

But I was Ceasorean born by Section – and have often wondered what the psychological effect was on my life 5/15/08

Enter the world.

Give yourself a few moments to experience this feeling.

Sense what this was like.

Experience yourself being born into this world.

What colors and shapes do you see?

What does your body feel like?

Now take yourself gradually back to yourself in the snapshot.

Draw yourself in the womb, yourself in the birth canal, at the moment of birth, in your snapshot, and as a speck of light.

This meditation helps bring up hidden parts of yourself that are unresolved or unacknowledged. These parts often hold a key part of the story of who we are and as such bring much to our creative process. Come back to this one often.

THE LEFT HAND

The first time I started to write in a book, I remember how awkward my hand felt. For the soft-lined books the teacher gave out, my left hand always reached out first. They let me use it. My father said that when he was in school his left hand was tied behind his back. The left hand was once considered bad. It's the shadow side. What would be in my left hand's shadow if I asked it to speak? Would there be the article I saw in the newspaper a few years ago about how left-handed people don't live as long as right-handed ones? Ever try using your left hand to cut with right-handed scissors? Or sitting at a school desk? Would my left hand's shadow be holding all the years of writing on pages, drawing in books, holding the carving mallet, putting on clothes, taking off clothes, combing my hair? What kind of memory does a hand hold?

Sometimes I think of myself as trying to touch a thought. What does a thought feel like? How would it be weighed? If I pulled it out of my brain, what kind of shape would it have? Would the left hand feel the shadow side, the "bad" side or would it be the same? Being left-handed may once have been like having red hair or freckles—a mark, a clear definition of difference, out of the norm. Being left-handed was once considered bad. Now it's just different.

5

Meditation and the Creative Mind

I walk through all the thoughts of my shadow,
I walk through my shadow in search of a moment.

OCTAVIO PAZ

When I carve wood, I often experience the wood as a person who is speaking to me. I listen to it, in a kind of "I-Thou" relationship. As the philosopher Martin Buber explains, there is an intimacy between ourselves and the things around us; in my case, between me and the wood. Recently, I read that the world-renowned potter Margaret Tafoya, from Santa Clara Pueblo in New Mexico, talked to her clay, called it "Mother Clay," and prayed to it before she shaped it into pots. It was easy for me to understand because of the way I work with the wood. Tewa, the language of Santa Clara, uses the same word, *nung*, to mean both *people* and *clay*. As potters work the clay, the pot and the person are intimately connected. The shape that becomes the pot embodies the spirit of both.

My friend, artist Lenore Tawney, was born in 1907. She is known for her collages and her weaving. Lenore is so youthful that I frequently forget her age, and we often chat as old friends about things of interest to us as contemporaries. I went to visit her recently and asked her about her spiritual connection to art. As I walk into her loft, which is both her studio and home, she tells me that a visitor recently told her that walking into her space is like walking into a prayer. The same visitor asked her if she strove for beauty in her work. "No," she said. "I strive for truth. It's all in my heart and my artmaking process. The artwork comes out like a great river." She chants mantras (prayers) all the time, all devoted to the Great Mother. One mantra is *Ham Sa*, "I am that, that is God." Another, her favorite, is *Om Namah Shivah*, which she translates as "I bow to the god within me."

Swami Chidvilsananda, the Siddha Yoga master, instructs us to honor ourselves with the same mantra. She translates *Om Namah Shivaya* a little differently, as "I honor the great primordial self within myself, awakening the conscious self to the vast eternal inner self." There is an interesting parallel here to talking to "Mother Clay."

Lenore was interested in the spiritual for as long as she can remember. She loved to go to vespers with her mother when she was little. Her first weaving was called *St. Francis and the Bird* and was dedicated to her father. She says that it was the beginning of her spiritual journey with art, her pilgrimage with it. It is as a pilgrim that Lenore sees herself on her journey in pursuit of truth. She recites the mantras on the route to find her artwork that "comes out like a great river."

The route in a pilgrimage is often rocky with many closed doors along the way. In my pilgrimage toward understanding, I grapple with one closed door after another. . But even when I finally unlock these doors, I often do not find much there immediately. Marcel Proust referred to memory as coming "like a rope let down from heaven" (Proust, pp. 5-6). Memory and experience exist like ghosts following you silently around without visible history. Reflecting on this, I began to ask myself, How could we in a workshop setting, or alone in our studios, go deeper in our exploration? How could we work more closely with the raw subject of ourselves? How could we find that primitive material buried there, our own internal rivers, that can help us change ourselves and our artwork?

Over many years, I have asked myself, how can I teach a way to find and listen and make art from that truth? I began to devise new workshops based in part on the Eastern philosophies that I had been studying, to experiment with the idea of combining meditation with artmaking. Guided meditation, according to the Vietnamese monk and Zen Master Thich Nhat Hanh, is an ancient technique from the time of the Buddha. With practice, your imagination becomes a window to your unconscious, to memory and experience. Participants in my workshops are able to do inner work at their own pace. Guided meditation, with its unfolding of the imagination, greets the unconscious. The idea is that your imagination and your unconscious can work together to bring to the surface gifts of wisdom and personal understanding. When applied to artmaking, a raw truth surfaces in the art.

Psychologist James Vargiu sees the connection between the creative and the meditative. He writes in his essay on creativity, "The classic stages of meditation—reflective meditation, receptive meditation, contemplation and discrimination—are quite parallel in nature to the stages of the creative process. Thus meditators can be seen as being creative workers and creative thinkers can be seen as practicing a definite kind of meditation. Such strong similarities between meditation and creative activity suggest that we are in fact dealing with two approaches to the same path of human development. These approaches although starting from very different points of departure, are in fact dealing with two approaches to the same path . . . toward the same goal: the development of a new mode of awareness and inner activity" (Vargiu, p. 41).

Tibetan Buddhism fosters a type of meditation called "sitting practice." It's a very simple activity. You sit and sit and you practice the art of being still on your chair or cushion, and you sit some more. And you breathe. The inhalation, the "in" breath, is involuntary and automatic. Following your "out" breaths, you observe the many facets of your mind. You become aware of what Chogyam Trungpa Rinpoche, one of my meditation teachers, calls the watcher, that part of yourself that watches you and makes reflective comments. The watcher is often the voice of sound judgment and encouragement, but it also can be the voice of the critic within.

Time and time again, I have found that the most direct way to begin to center myself and connect with my inner world and the spaciousness of the mind, and to transcend that inner critic, is by sitting still. Many of us never take the time to do this, and even when we do, find it excruciating to sit by ourselves quietly without distraction. If you have never meditated, take five minutes and just sit and follow your breath. Every time a thought arises, as it will almost immediately, just note it without judgment and allow your attention to return to the out breath. As you become aware of the exhalation, let your awareness travel out into space and dissolve as the breath does. Slowly, you will discover your inner chitchat settling down.

With the practice of noting my breath, becoming aware of my breathing, I discovered the spaces between my thoughts. This was a surprise to me because I had believed that constant thinking was an essential part of living. In fact, I thought I would die if I did not think. Yet, as I sat and breathed, I could watch the place where the in breath ended and the out breath began. That moment was the "no thought" moment that gave me a sense of spaciousness, of openness. It was the very moment that was the "crack between the worlds" as described in this Native American prayer. The opening where the artwork "comes out like a great river" as Lenore Tawney described in her process. Watching the ebb and flow of your breath, you learn about your own nature and your thinking/no thinking process, and you learn about the entrance to the creative process.

Native American Prayer
Sundancer, dance into the light
We give our whole being to open up our sight
That we might see the vision, every landscape unfold
That we might dance through the crack between the worlds.
—*from* 30 Offerings, *a selection of Native American Prayers in the collection of Joan Halifax, a Buddhist teacher and anthropologist*

Mind's Eye, Taking Beautiful Breaths

This meditation is a beginning, a good way to start to become familiar with the gift of your breath, to begin to be aware of it, to watch it, and to imagine yourself as a being of breath. Each time you do this meditation, you will see your drawings change. After a while you might want to add the experience of watching the ebb and flow of your breath and to locate "the crack between the worlds" in your breathing.

Breathe and breathe.

Our breath is the source of our life.

It purifies and clears our lungs and gives oxygen to the cells in our bodies.

Breathe again.

Many of us hold our breath or breathe in a shallow way.

Keep this idea in your mind as you proceed, filling your lungs fully and emptying them fully.

Breathing in and out, in and out.

Imagine yourself with your out breath gliding on the wings of your beautiful bird.

Each out breath gliding on beautiful wings.

Try taking deep breaths.

Now imagine these breaths going down into your feet.

Now out through your toes.

Now imagine bringing up the breath to your shoulders and your head.

Rest there for a moment, continuing to take deep breaths.

Breathing in and out, in and out.

Now bring your breath down to your hands and to your fingertips.

Imagine yourself breathing out through your hands.

See yourself in your mind's eye filling your whole body with luminous breath, your breath.

You are filled with the beauty of your breath completely inside of you.

What does it feel like?

Watch yourself be with your breath.

See the breath outside of you, all around you as well as within you until you become a being of breath.

Stay with that for a moment.

Just let yourself sit with it.

Relax into yourself as a being filled with breath.

Now bring your breath to your heart.

Stay at your heart for a moment, watching your breath from your heart.

Now draw a mental picture of your breath, and see if you can give it a color, a shape, and form.

Draw whatever comes to mind. Don't censor it.

Create a mental picture of your breath.

Yoga teacher Marcia Albert calls it "riding the wings of breath."

You are now ready to draw your breath on the wings of your bird.

Drawing an In Breath and an Out Breath

Follow your breathing for several in and out breaths. On an 11x14 sheet of paper, draw a line that divides the sheet into two parts. Divide it any way you like. One part will be for your in breath and one for your out breath.

From your watercolors, choose one color for your in breath and another for your out breath. Dip your brush in water, then fill it with the in-breath color and place it lightly on the in-breath side of the paper. Breathe in, allowing the brush to move as you inhale. Let the stroke express the sensation of your in breath. Spend a moment looking at it.

Rinse your brush and fill it with the out-breath color. Put the brush on the out-breath side of the paper and exhale, trying to follow that sensation with the stroke of the brush. Continue to work with the rhythm of your breath, letting your brush express it on paper.

Now see both sides of your breath on the page. Bring your attention to the dividing line between in and out and, in your breathing, to the point just after you have exhaled and before you draw another breath. Hold that place for a moment. What color and shape would express your suspended breath? Select a color and put it on your page in a way that expresses the feeling.

You now have a complete picture of your breath.

Working With the Light, Rainbow Light

This meditation is a way to bring spirit light into your breath. Sometimes called a rainbow light by meditators, it is used as a healing source and as an access to wisdom by many cultures—from the Holy Ghost in Christianity, illustrated as a halo in paintings, to the Hindu idea of a ray of light as the source of all wisdom. We all have a rainbow light. (Kirlian photography, a technique developed by two Russians for photographing the aura, captures this light as it emanates from plants and humans.)

Breathe and relax and breathe and relax.

Imagine a white light at the top of your head. (When we use

white light in this kind of work we mean that all the colors of the rainbow come together to make white light, the way sunlight does.)

Visualize a white light above the top of your head at your crown, and breathe and relax and breathe and relax.

Let yourself stay there for a moment.

Just spend a moment there with it, breathing in and out, using your breath together with your light, and releasing any tension in yourself.

Relax, relax, relax.

Let the light fill your body.

Notice yourself breathing with it.

Imagine yourself touching your light.

How does it feel to touch your light?

What kind of weight does it have?

What kind of texture?

Let it rest in your hands for a few minutes, see how that feels.

Now ask yourself where does your light usually stay in your body?

How does it feel there? Get a good look at where that is.

Make a mental note of it.

See your light in your hand.

Breathe with your light into your hand out through your fingertips. Now bring it back through your body, your whole body down to your toes, up through your legs to the base of the spine, and breathe and relax, relax and breathe there.

Now take your light, and bring it up to the top of your head.

Let it hover there for a few minutes.

Draw the experience of your light.

Describe in your drawing what your light looks like.

Painting the Rainbow Light

With your mind's eye, imagine a rainbow. Draw this rainbow with as many of the colors of the rainbow as you can. Your rainbow may look like a "rainbow"—that is, the conventional red, orange, yellow, green, indigo, and violet order—or may not. It is your rainbow and can look any way that you please.

Now look at your rainbow. Where is it placed on your page? How big is it? How much on the page does it occupy? What feelings come up as you look at your rainbow? Look at its colors, its shape. Become familiar with it. Imagine your rainbow all around you. This is your rainbow light.

THE TAP SHOES

The tap shoes. I remember looking at them over and over. I remember taking them out of the box and touching their perky black ribbons. Staring at the shine on the pumps and turning them over and looking at the taps under them, those shiny metal parts under the sole at the tip and heel. They were so beautiful. Then I would put them back into the box and put them in the closet, close the door, and leave them there. A few minutes later I would come back and repeat the whole thing. Take the box out of the closet, open it, look at the shiny black patent, rub my palm across it, and thrill to the smooth surface—a little cool and indifferent to the touch—and to the ribbon lying out from the eyelet on the side, with just the perfect wrinkle from where the bow went. This is it. I am eight years old and bursting with the chance to wear these shoes and to make noise with them, to play the patterns of the sounds, to "Shuffle Off to Buffalo."

I wonder what happened to them. They are still with me, wherever they are. I remember slipping my foot into them, and how my foot welcomed them. It felt like Cinderella's glass slipper, but only in the quiet of my room. The silence there with the shoes and the door closed. Putting them on quietly and imagining the soft tapping becoming louder and louder as I charged from the room into a magical place with only open doors and no one to say anything. I could just imagine myself tapping for hours, hours, the rhythmical sounds bringing, keeping me away.

What are you doing? she says. Put that away, she says. What nonsense, she says. What do you think that you are trying to do? Make a fool out of me with your pleasure. Put those back in their box. I'm sorry I bought them for you. Can't you see that you are daydreaming the day away and that nothing is getting done? You were supposed to get ready for your bath and you haven't even finished your homework. You are a naughty bad girl who doesn't have any appreciation for anyone except herself.

And I slave all day, she said. Slave all day so that you can be such an ungrateful girl and spend all of her time with these damn shoes. If I had a mind to it, I would throw them out the window and then you would be really really sorry. Wouldn't you? Then you would have no shoes any more. Who cares about your dancing? What is this dance teacher to me? She's just a good-for-nothing. I bet she doesn't slave to keep a little girl, to feed and clothe her the way that I do. To iron and wash and spend all of my time cooking, and for what? For you to dance around, to put these shoes on all of the time instead of being sensible, looking after your chores, making your mother happy. Now get to work and finish your homework and then get ready for your bath. And put those damn shoes back in their box and get them into the closet as soon as you can, or I will take them away from you for good. That's good, just leave them there, and don't take them out until I tell you to. I will make the decision when you can wear them again since I'm your mother and what I say goes.

It felt like sand.

It felt like a knife in the heart.

It felt like a wound in the eye.

It felt like a stab in the toe.

It felt that deafness overcame her.

It felt like the shoes would never fit.

6

Healing the Inner Critic

I certainly had no feeling for harmony, and Schoenberg thought
that that would make it impossible for me to write music. He
said, "You'll come to a wall you won't be able to get through."
So I said, I'll beat my head against that wall.

JOHN CAGE

When my daughter, Nana, was in the third grade, her school notebook was confiscated because the teacher discovered her drawing
in it in the library. School rules did not permit this. I was called into
school to discuss, in front of her no less, how Nana could be so bad
and unruly as to draw in her notebook in the library. I was horrified.
While I could understand the teacher's concern about children mark-
ing up library books, it seemed harsh to make a child feel bad by
removing her instrument of communication and pleasure in such a
cruel manner. Painfully, I remember Nana sitting there completely
perplexed because the confiscation was against everything she had
learned at home. She loved her pencils and markers, expressing her
creativity in images as well as in words. Fortunately, she was not
deterred by this incident later in life. In fact, she says that she does-
n't even remember the incident. She became an artist.

Not everyone is as fortunate. Many people coming to this process
of artmaking, as I have witnessed in my workshops, often feel frozen
because they were stopped in their childhood from exploring their
personal images. I remember Julie, who by the third day of our
workshop couldn't stop weeping. She was remembering a teacher
who had humiliated her by holding up to the class her little draw-

ing of a tree, using it as an example of how not to make a tree. After recalling this memory, Julie opened up. She had wanted for a long time to make art, but she just couldn't figure out why, when she got to her worktable, she would put everything ahead of artmaking, remembering, for example, all of her undone tasks, which suddenly became urgent.

Julie was judging herself. Her inner critic had overpowered her beginner's mind. Her inner critic had become that unenlightened teacher. In all of us, the inner critic is sure to surface sooner or later in similar ways. It says to us, "Don't do it." "It's wrong." "Abandon it." "Throw it away."

Voices like this make you feel bad, incompetent, and lost. You end up thinking: "Everybody else has the potential to make wonderful things—paintings, drawings, sculptures—but not me. It will never happen." That inner critic has a way of distracting you. It encourages you instead to go for a walk, do the laundry, take a nap, pay your bills. Some of this distraction can be a positive part of the creative process in that while doing these other tasks your ideas—ideas that are not coming forth fluidly—begin to percolate. Allowing the critic to caution you is helpful and positive, but if you allow it to destroy your process, you halt your own creative passion.

In my workshops I tell those who have made art to think of this workshop as a new and fresh experience for making art. And to those who have never made art, I suggest they express themselves as if they were children. Let go of past attitudes and experiences that have put you in a position of making things that aren't from the heart. Allow yourself to open to the possibilities that everything is possible. People who have never painted before are often surprised at how much they can do.

Author and psychologist Jack Kornfield suggests sitting in silence (in upright meditation posture if desired), watching the different judgments that come up during the course of an hour or so, and then acknowledging and speaking to them. "Thank you, Dad," "I heard what you said, Mrs. Smith, but I wonder how you know?" By doing this practice, you can develop an awareness as to how to enlist the critic to become your friend and ally rather than your adversary. The idea of making your inner critic your friend is an essential part of this process toward change. Once you see this voice within you as fully part of you and as an ally, it becomes an important part of your artmaking process, an ally of suggestion and dialogue affording constructive criticism and helping you along the way.

Let me go back for a moment to my father, who used to say about my abstract organic sculpture, "Why don't you for just once make something that looks like something." I would always struggle to respond. Once, I said, "Dad, maybe you can think about your dreams and see that I am making forms that you might find there." Perplexed, he responded, "You have very strange dreams." Shortly after my father died, I had a vision of him in which he came back to me and he said, "Now I understand what you make."

Finding Your Child Within

This meditation can help you connect to your creative inner child, the child whose world began to shape the inner critic.

Relax in a comfortable chair, sitting with your back straight.

Go back in time to find yourself as a child, your own personal child self.

See her in your mind's eye and bring her out into the light.

See her in this light.

How old is she?

What is she wearing? Look down at her feet. What are her shoes like?

Get acquainted with her.

What kind of child is this?

Is she happy?

What kind of life does she have?

Does she feel wanted, comfortable?

See your child playing. Let her bring you there to her playful place. What is she doing?

Watch her play.

See her drawing a picture of her world for you.

See the picture develop. Get a good look at it.

Now ask your child to speak to you.

Ask her to tell you something about herself, to give you a message about how she feels about herself.

What would she like you to know?

Now ask her, your child, a question about herself? What would you like to know about her?

Let her tell you. Just be silent with yourself and listen to her.

Drawing Your Child Within

Surround yourself with your crayons and drawing pad and begin to draw with them. Be a child and play with the colors and shapes. Scribble on the paper, if you dare. Break your crayons in two if you like and remove the paper around them. Use these crayons on their side to made wide strokes across the pad, or use only the points. Make many marks on the paper, varying the lengths and widths. Consider the whole paper. Don't forget the edges and corners of the pad. Let the crayons go off the pad if you feel like it. Overlap your colors.

Now draw your child.

Draw the picture that she made for you.

Draw her world as she has shown it to you and capture her message—if you can.

THE FLOWER OPENS

Lying in the mud I wanted the flowers to open. I was frightened that my mother would see me lying there all dirty, but I was not moving an inch, hoping that the soft thick rain would make the petals open, and then I would finally see how it happened. Each day I would come down outside and check the petals. The rosebud would have already opened and I would be perplexed as to why. I didn't see it. I guess it was like my child's body growing without me seeing it, or even feeling it. The rain kept coming, and I watched and waited like a hunter stalking its prey. Someone had told me that the rain made the flowers grow, and here I was at last waiting and watching. By now, I was sinking into the grass as the rain got stronger.

I sensed the slight movement of a person in the house at the window and realized it was my grandmother watching me. I looked up and she was calling me to come in, looking very stern and grave. I was afraid to ignore her. In my Sicilian culture my grandmother rarely spoke directly to me. She would tell my mother in front of me to tell me something. When she did speak to me, she had to be listened to. So I ran in through her door and let her shake me dry like a cat. She told me that I would die of the wet. No one cared about my experiment, least of all her in her white starched dry apron.

I was placed on a counter and my clothes were removed one at a time. My grandmother mumbled about what my mother would think. I was getting cold, almost blue in the lips, and beginning to shake, some from fear, some from the cold. What will she do now, I thought, as she wrapped me in a towel?

Oh, the memory comes back. I wasn't punished because my mother wasn't home and I was in my grandmother's charge, so instead I was wrapped in a towel and scowled at. I didn't see the flowers open and I despaired that I never would. The secrets, the mystery, the magic wasn't for me, I thought. What if everyone else has seen these roses open and I can't? What does that mean about me? And now I am thinking where was my mother, where did she go?

I hadn't seen her for a while. Maybe my brother was being born. Maybe that's why I was watching those flowers to see how they too were born, and I failed. But I didn't tell anyone, not a word, because they all knew about flowers and babies, and I was not in on the mystery.

7

Cultivating the Imagination

An artist works because he must! But he learns by the
disciplines of his imagination. Through moments of ecstasy or
great despair, when all thoughts of self are lost, a work seems
to evolve which has not only the vivid uniqueness of a new
creation, but also the seeming effortlessness and unalterable
simplicity of a true idea relating to the universe.

BARBARA HEPWORTH

In my studio, on this sunny morning, I want to begin a new work.
I place my log from a fir tree in front of me and sit with it. We sit as
if we are two very old friends who don't need to say anything in
each other's presence and whose presence is comforting to each
other. I imagine the tree that this log came from as I sit with it, the
kind of life it had. I listen with my sketchpad on my lap until I make
a mark on the page or onto the wood. The first mark usually brings
the second and so on. The images come with the mark, forged from
sensation, from memory pressed into myself, images that I retrieve
time and again. There is an endless supply from my grandfather's
garden, shadows large and small, voices and faces, the shape of
someone's neck, the names of childhood friends, a fairy tale someone read to me, the gesture of a smile, a conversation about
yesterday's dinner.

These images can become hands traced, pressed and carved on
wood panels. They become an eight-foot sculpture of repeated hand-
prints, bright red over and over, carved into a gold panel, called
Hand Wall. Or, at another time, they are destined to become a bigger-
than-life coat, called *Great Coat*—the kind my grandfather wore in
the 1940s to envelop himself in warmth, now carved into wood ten

feet tall, gilded bright as sunlight, two tree limbs like arms hugging the coat. I can conjure up my past, tucked away in my imagination, and examine what is there, going through my mind as if it were a trunk in an attic, for the little surprises and gems in my memory that are part of my history, giving depth and richness, authenticity and spirit to my work.

This particular morning, I think about how many times over the years I have been at the beginning of the process of making sculpture, and how hard it has been to find the doorway into that personal place of my imagination. Early on it was grinding work, years of feeling lost, until I began to realize that this, too, was part of the creative process to be sought out and honored. There were times when I would stop working in my beautiful sunny studio and go to work in a dark cavelike room. The brilliant sun of the studio drove me out of it. I needed to hide in this cavelike room for weeks until I felt as if I were at the bottom of a mineshaft and began to see some light there.

Here in my imagination are these unique pictures, images, sounds, colors, words that only I could have, and they are waiting to come to the surface if I wait and listen. Listening—what Barbara Hepworth called the discipline of the imagination—is key to the process of artmaking. Appreciating it is the first step in opening the "door" to creativity. One of my students calls it "mining the gold."

Intention—"I intend," "I desire," "I will it" —begins to open the channel to my imagination. It is my intention to make something, my intention that calls forth the idea, the shape, the spirit that takes form. By using memory as an archive and imagination as my inspiration, my art can develop without a formula. Each memory image surprises and delights because it arises from within and belongs unquestionably to me, the maker. I am convinced that this is the place from which all the great masters worked, and it is accessible to all of us.

The artist Magritte made a painting of a seated man in a bowler hat and a suit missing a middle section from his heart to the center of his torso. In its place was a white dove in a cage. There was a photo of it on the cover of the magazine section of the Sunday newspaper when I was a teenager. When I saw it, I felt a wonderful, instant connection because it expressed how I felt about my world, in a way I had never seen it expressed before. I still remember the first time I saw it. I wanted to be that person who made it.

Making art is instinctive, like learning to speak in words. There are ancient cave paintings and rock carvings on every continent. Perhaps our imagination desires this visual language, or perhaps it is because our imagination gives access to spirit, and by making art we can feel a tangible connection to spirit that is otherwise so intangible.

One of the most exciting parts of my teaching experience over the years has been that I have never seen one student make an image that is exactly the same as another's image; no two paintings or sculptures are alike. There may be a relationship, but the artwork of two people is never identical. Here in this place is the unique and magical difference of our persons. Yet I constantly hear students dismissing their work and their process: "It was just my imagination," or "My imagination is odd to me, I don't know where it comes from." Students have also bemoaned their lack of imagination: "I don't have any imagination and therefore I cannot make art." "That didn't really happen, it was just my imagination."

This distrust of imagination comes because essentially we have been taught to trust our reason and to be suspicious of any other approach to ideas. While there is a small window for our intuition, sometimes referred to as a hunch or a bright idea, thinking outside of our usual frame of reference or our usual ways of expressing information is largely discredited in our everyday life.

Yet respecting our imaginations is part of an old tradition. The ancient Greeks thought that the very first drawing was created by a young woman. Yearning to be with her lover when he was gone, she traced the outline of his shadow on her wall to keep his presence with her. Earlier, the Egyptians instructed a spiritual seeker to find an image by making a drawing of the God Besa on his left hand and enveloping the hand in a strip of black cloth that had been consecrated to the Goddess Isis. I imagine this inspired the supplicant to honor his hand as an instrument of the divine, the image on his hand becoming the key, even the bridge to the images that lay awaiting inside him.

Many ancient and not so ancient peoples believed that the imagination was a separate faculty of our existence and that it had its own realm within us. Sixteenth-century scholar and physician Paracelsus wrote, "the imagination is like the sun. The sun has a light which is not tangible; but which nevertheless may set a house on fire. . . . The great truth of the universe lies within the human imagination."(Ackroyd, p. 148). And in the eighteenth-century, painter, poet, and visionary William Blake, whose writings were inspired by Paracelsus, wrote that the imagination, "liveth forever."(Ackroyd, p. 149). There are many other references. The great Islamic mystics thought there was a world of image, an intermediary between the realm of intellect and that of sense perception. The French poet Baudelaire called imagination the "queen of truth"(Baudelaire, in *Art in Theory*, pp. 489-490). The philosopher John Ruskin referred to the imagination as "the highest faculty of the human mind . . . when toiling in the presence of things that cannot be dealt with by any other power"(Ruskin, p. 88). Recently I read about a prisoner in New York state, an artist, who said that his imagination was a solace to him, a sacred place, a faculty of being that helped him to travel far beyond the confines of his prison bars.

The concept of concrete reality to the over thirty million tribal people living in India is far different from our own. Stella Kramrisch, curator of Indian Art at the Philadelphia Museum of the Arts in the 1960s, noted that the living world of these tribal people is a combination of waking experience, trance, and dream. That is to say, they see their imagination as part and parcel of their everyday existence. It is through their art—wood carvings, large papier-mâché sculptures, wall paintings, brightly colored floor diagrams, painted cloth, huge clay altars—that they are able to give "form to their reality expressing itself . . . directly in rites in which works of art are the indispensable and focal means of communication . . . with their [experience] of what they call the real"(Kramrisch, p. 50).

In Tibetan Buddhist practice, the practitioner uses the imagination to create and then fully enter into an idealized experience of divine energies. In this way imagination and divine reality meet and are manifested in sacred paintings called *thangkas*, which are the visual representations of these energies. By meditating on these images and recreating them in the mind, the practitioner is able to receive insight that expands the dimension of the known self.

Many modern Western health professionals are now using imagination as an instrument to healing. The work of such proponents as Bernie Siegel, Carolyn Myss, Deepak Chopra, and Jeanne Achterberg has brought the awareness of the relationship between mind, body, and spirit to the medical field at large. James Vargiu, a psychosynthesist psychologist writing in the 1970s, eloquently described the connection between emotions and the imagination: "By the purposeful utilization of mental images and symbols, we can release blocked emotional energy, transform it when released, and also develop or evoke feelings which are most in tune with our best values and goals (e.g. serenity, harmony, beauty, joy, courage, and so forth.)"(Vargiu, p. 29).

These ideas have directly shaped a weeklong workshop that I teach called "Artmaking as an Act of Healing" in which we explore different energy centers in the body through the power of our imaginations. From the insights gleaned from this work we make drawings and paintings. In truth, the approach is ancient, even in Western culture. In the Gnostic Gospels, the Book of Thomas attributes the following quote to Jesus: "If you bring forth what is within you, what you bring forth will save you. If you do not bring forth what is within you, what you do not bring forth will destroy you" (Pagels, p. XV).

Opening the Doors to Two Rooms Within Yourself

This meditation and exercise uses the idea of two rooms to explore your imaginative spirit. Each room represents either an outer layer or an inner layer. The first room is an anteroom of people and influences, while the second room takes you deeper into the dwelling place of your own images. Return to these rooms time and again to refresh and replenish your imagination. Draw them many times. Begin by imagining yourself opening one closed door after another.

The First Room

Sit quiet and still and relaxed.

Follow your breath, watching yourself breathing in and out.

Now imagine a door in front of you.

Think of this door as a very old door to a room that contains your imagination.

Notice the door.

How big it is?

What it is made out of?

How it is attached to the room?

What color it is?

Very gently open the door and look inside.

What do you see in the room there?

This room is a metaphor for your imagination.

What is the inside of this room of your imagination like?

What kind of a room is it?

What does it contain?

What are the walls like?

What colors are they?

Take a good look.

Are there any windows?

How is it furnished?

Get to know this room and begin to feel comfortable with it.

Imagine yourself inside it, looking around.

Now put some people in your room with you.

See them there, in this room of your imagination.

How many people besides yourself have you put into the room?

Look at them. Do you know them?

Who are they?

And how are they connected to your imagination?

Spend some time with your visitors.

Ask them to tell you about themselves.

What would they like to tell you?

What would they like you to know?

Let yourself listen carefully.

Draw the door and the room.

And what and who is within it.

The Second Room

Using your mind's eye, find the door to a second room.

This room holds the images of your imagination.

Notice the door to your second room.

How is the door made?

What is its height and color?

The door is locked.

Find the key for it and unlock it.

How does it open?

Now open the door and enter this second room.

Opening this second door, notice the inside of the door.

See what kind of images are on it.

You are now inside of this imaginary second room.

Once you are inside, look around your room.

Walk around in it.

Look at yourself in this room.

How old you are?

What you are wearing?

Now notice what kind of images are there for you.

Are the walls painted?

What kind of furniture is there?

Are there symbols? Slogans?

Other things to know about yourself?

Note the shapes and forms of these images and their texture.

Touch them with your mind's hand.

If the walls could speak, what would they say to you?

In this room of your imagination find an image that represents your creative spirit.

Give your spirit a shape and color and form.

What does it look like?

Let yourself get to know it by touching it, looking at it, or talking to it.

Have you seen it before?

Does it remind you of someone or something?

Draw this room.

Draw its door.

Draw yourself in it.

Draw what is inside of the room.

Draw your creative spirit.

Give a presence to your images when you are drawing them.

Make up whatever you can to add to your drawings if you like.

THE BLACK CUSHION

I will always have this memory. I would like it to go away, because it is a memory of something I would prefer not to hold, but I know it won't go away. It's about a black round cushion that I had for years. It had a few stains on it and a bit of red paint as well. I used it to do Buddhist meditation practice. It was in fact a Zen cushion, but I usually practice a kind of Tibetan meditation so already it was an oddity. I have always been an oddity myself, and my cushion was like me in that way. (Tibetan cushions are yellow and orange and squarer and higher; mine was dark, black like a crow, and round and plump.) It was also a bit hard so that sitting on it was a challenge, especially for long periods of time.

I brought this cushion to a workshop recently and sat on its hard body for hours and hours, breathing in and out and listening to myself. When I returned to it after a break, it was gone. One of the 550 people there had taken my cushion. It was such an ordinary Zen cushion that it was hard to find mine among the other homely, black, plump cushions. I looked and looked but finally had to borrow someone else's cushion.

What do I really care about this cushion? It represents a loss to me, a loss of something that was mine and had my energy and was a companion and friend to look at and sit on all these years. What an irony! Here in this workshop I was supposed to learn how to give up attachment, and yet I am attached to this hard round cushion to the point of searching everywhere for it. Searching so hard that when I thought that I had found it, I was sure that everything would be okay. I was so sure that it was my cushion. The voice inside of me said, "You've found it. It has your stains on it."

So at last I had come to my cushion after searching for it and looking at all the other round Zen cushions there that were not common, yet just common enough. There were just enough of them to make the search a challenge. And then I discovered others were stained in the same way that mine was.

This realization made my heart flutter. It felt like a feather. It quivered. It brought up this memory where I saw myself as a child being in a room with adults who were so big that I only saw their legs. They were talking to each other and didn't notice that I was there, and no matter what I did they patted me on the head and kept talking to each other. I had to be just short of irritating them. I used to know how far to go to get to that point—just how far to go before stopping, like trying to get your feet wet in the puddle outside when you have been told not to. To just set your foot in for a moment, let the water seep in just enough and then pull it out. How is this like the cushion? Sitting on a black plump cushion that holds my back and spine straight brings up memories that float around in my mind. It takes me again and again to this puddle where I can test my mind in order to have a clear vision of what is.

So that's what it is. This cushion holds, held, all of those memories, and since I have taken someone else's cushion that I was convinced was mine, I have theirs, not mine. Someone else is sitting on my cushion, getting their feet wet.

8

Truth and Myth about Being an Artist

The uninitiated imagine that one must await inspiration in order to create. That is a mistake. I am far from saying that there is no such thing as inspiration: quite the opposite. It is found as a driving force in every human activity and is in no wise peculiar to artists. But that force is only brought into action by an effort, and that effort is work . . .it is not simply inspiration that counts; it is the result of inspiration.

IGOR STRAVINSKY

Artmaking is a natural endeavor, so very ordinary and so much a birthright for each of us. Tibetan Buddhist Master Pema Chodron writes about spiritual practice, "all of us are eagles who have forgotten how to fly"(Chodron, p. 141). I think this also applies to our approach to art. We all can make art if we allow ourselves, but the myth that artists are born not made stops many of us from trying. The simple truth is that making art is hard work. Moreover, American artists are not integrated into our society as are artists in other cultures, like the tribal artist in India, or the potter from the Santa Clara Pueblo in New Mexico. In our society, we are usually set apart as someone different. And it is hard not to be put off by the myth of specialness surrounding the artist in our culture, because there are so many misconceptions about artists, not the least being that the great artist is born a genius, isolated and separate from everyone else.

If we can try out our "wings" and make a commitment to pursue this path, we have to grapple with the concept of how an artist fits into our culture. Contrary to the popular idea, the artist's life is not like the one described in the movie *Pollock*, in which Jackson Pollock is portrayed as going to parties, getting drunk, and then entering his studio and in a flash making a great painting. It doesn't make a great movie to tell the truth about the process, but making art can be grinding work. It is interesting and exciting, but a commitment to artmaking requires hard work and discipline, imagination and perseverance. It also requires thought, contemplation, often research, and much trial and error before the artist can translate what she wants to say into a visual format, a painting or sculpture, a movie, or an installation.

Some artists try to live out the myths. There are many artists I have known personally who tried to drink like Jackson Pollock to improve their art. I don't think it helped much. When I was a young artist, I was often discouraged because older artists would talk about how easy it was for them, and this was so far away from the process that I knew in my studio. There were moments when the work would flow, but more times than not it didn't, and I would have to struggle with the hard work of it. It was only later that I realized the older artists were stretching the truth to keep the myth going for themselves.

It takes time to develop the discipline to make art. At the beginning I had the will to become an artist and some encouragement from my teacher, but no discipline to go into my studio routinely. I did not know how to bring myself to the discipline of looking for the path. Little by little, I would spend just a few minutes each day in my art space. Even if I wasn't inspired, I would just sit there in my studio. At the same time I would try to train myself to think about what I was working on each day during breaks from routine activities such as child rearing, teaching, domestic chores, and so forth. Gradually, I was able to set aside mornings as the time for work, even if I only had an hour or two before going to my other jobs. The results came slowly, but they inspired me to continue.

Sculptor Barbara Hepworth raised triplets during World War II. In her pictorial autobiography, she writes: "I made a firm foundation for my working life, and it formed my idea that a woman artist is not deprived by cooking and having children, nor by nursing children with measles (even in triplicate)—one is in fact nourished by this rich life, provided one always does some work each day;

even a single half hour, so that the images grow in one's mind"(Hepworth, p. 20).

My daughter, Nana, now in her early thirties, decided to become a painter at the age of eighteen, although she stopped making art for a while in her late twenties. She said the biggest obstacle for her was fear, the fear of making "bad" art. " I was always worried what other people thought, and this was getting in my way. I changed my mind after stopping for a while, because I was unhappy. There was this incredible pull to make art when I stopped. I struggled to believe in my voice, to acknowledge its truth. I found that the most important part of artmaking was the making, and that the process was what I learned the most from. It was the means to the end of being human, and I didn't feel alone anymore. The part that I enjoy about painting is that while I am making it I travel. I feel as if I am moving through time and space in a different way."

When I asked her to describe the travel, she replied, "Travel is being in nothingness. It encapsulates life. Being able in some way to convey my dreams, which before that moment are unknown to me. It makes me feel alive and one with every other aspect of the universe. That's what makes art fantastic. It is that wonderful jelling together in harmony."

My friend Gayla thinks she stopped painting for years because when she was in art school, she became so immersed in the artwork that she lost a sense of herself and became frightened. No one told her that becoming lost was a natural part of becoming found, and a good way to connect to spirit.

There is a kind of radiance that permeates a great work of art. Talent is the ability to translate this radiance, to put this radiance on a canvas or wall or in a log that reaches out to us. Talent comes from opening yourself up to being sensitive to experience, making the creative journey, and following that vision. It is true that some people can easily draw very well realistically, or have an innate ability to put colors together. Neither of those came easily to me, but I found that I had a really good sense of composition and was able to place the forms together in a way that made people take notice.

Maybe that is another part of what talent is, the ability to reach someone else—the viewer, listener, audience—to touch them, to have them take notice. When this happens, we say that this is a talented person, that their radiance comes through and reaches out to us. That radiance can be called spirit, the way it takes form is called talent, and each of us has access to it in some form.

WORKING BY THE SEAT OF MY PANTS

What an odd description, to see myself taking the seat of my pants and moving them around. Is it sitting in these different metaphorical chairs, moving around, that brings me to the making of art? Is it about the stillness, the emptiness, the vastness, the openness with no one there? I am literally there, but I don't remember that I know her, this person who is me. She's not the person that I am acquainted with, but at that moment I don't care. I have just dropped down into a deep place, and there is no one home, not even myself. Then there comes something, something no longer familiar, but not too unfamiliar. Whatever it is, it feels sort of connected to someone, something, somewhere inside. It is the beginning, the first step of many steps when it begins to lead to something. Each shape, each form, each color leads to the next.

There is still no one home. I do not have a sense of myself and feel unacquainted with her. If I take the time to look, there is only an empty space. Now that empty place takes a little shape, and little by little, I walk back and look at it and find it saying something to me. Homeless as I feel, there is this place that is calling me to come in and be in it. Now is the time for a kind of standing back and looking to decide whether or not to be drawn in. Of course, there is no choice. I must do it. I know it as it calls me. But I feel the fear, the edge, the limits of every moment in the past until this moment. I have never gone this far before. This is the way it feels, and each and every time is a variation on it. Of course, there is no choice. I must continue. I am at sea in a flimsy boat trying to steer my way through without a compass or guide. Well, maybe the wood (or canvas) is a guide, but that's it. This is the way it feels each and every time.

Today my art is inseparable from my spiritual practice. I have discovered ways to feel the divine in myself by making my art as an expression of the unknown and a route to healing. I hope that you will make that so for yourself and make your art with spirit.

Make a special place for yourself, be it a corner of a room, or a full-fledged studio. Bring magical things there: a feather, a stone, a flower, and set aside time for yourself to be there. Make it sacred.

Open your doors. Put on your wings.

part two

MEDITATIONS and EXERCISES

9

Short Meditations

There is a story from India about a doll made of salt who went in search of God. When it dove into the ocean, dissolving completely, its quest was fulfilled.

SHRI ANANDI MA, KUNDALINI MAHA YOGA MASTER

Recently, a friend asked me to describe the process of artmaking as a spiritual practice, and I wrote this for her: I sit and sit in the silence, looking hard into the blankness and wait and wait quietly for my hand to bring me a form, for my heart to speak to me and for spirit to surface. In making art we use our bodies and our minds, our hearts and our spirit. Spirit, once it comes, sits on our shoulders and gives us vision and presence, brings form, and speaks to the spiritual practice of artmaking. When spirit takes form, the healing properties and magical qualities inherent in artmaking take shape, holding its presence in the work of art, and speaking to the viewer with its radiance.

Discovering Your Instrument

While I make many artworks using hands, I made one particular sculpture inspired by my early childhood years of learning to use my hands. *Child's Hand Box*, made in 1999, is a small golden box with many red carved child's hands pressed into the wood. When you open the box, it is painted red inside like the hands outside. I think of it as embodying the spirit of a child self, innocent, curious, open. Your hand is an instrument of yourself, your own instrument of healing, of making, of caring, of tenderness and love. This meditation gives you an opportunity to connect to an early experience of your hands and to the memories stored there. Do it often. It will give you many memories to draw.

Imagine your light coming down through your body.

Illuminating your whole body, making your inner body radiant.

Now bring this radiant light to your hands.

To your left hand.

And to your right hand.

And now to both hands.

As you imagine your light going through each hand, pay attention to how it feels.

Look at your left hand.

Imagine the light flowing through it.

Notice what that is like.

See if there is any place that feels tight and release the tension there. Get familiar with the character and nature of your left hand.

Notice the lines in it.

The shape of your fingers, your palm.

Now go to your right hand.

Imagine your light flowing through it.

Notice what that is like, again paying attention to how it feels.

See if there is any place that feels tight and release the tension there.

Get familiar with the character and nature of your right hand.

Notice the lines in it.

The shape of your fingers, your palm.

What kind of information do your hands hold?

What is the earliest memory that your hands have in them?

Let your hands tell you.

What are you doing in this memory?

Who is there?

How old are you?

See your hands bringing you this memory.

What is it your hands would like you to know from this memory?

What would your right hand tell your left hand if it could?

What would your left hand tell your right hand if it could?

How are your hands in your life for you?

How do they serve you?

Trace your hands.

And now draw what memories that they would like you to know.

Spirit Taking Form

This straightforward meditation will help you begin to give shape and voice to your spirit, help your spirit to take form. Spirit is not a material presence, of course, but we are trying to glimpse it in our mind's eye, to see if we can find an image for it.

Begin with your light.

Imagine it at the top of your head going down through your body.

See yourself breathing with your light.

Find your inner self with your mind's eye and take it to the place of spirit. (If nothing comes to mind just make it up.)

What color is it? What does it look like? What kind of texture does it have?

How big is it? How is it held in your body? Where is it held in your body?

Let it speak to you.

What would it like to tell you?

Make a note in your mind of what it says and ask it some questions.

Ask it why it has taken this form within you.

Ask it if it is like anyone you know.

Ask it if it will help you on your journey in your life, and with your artmaking process.

Draw your spirit. Draw where it resides within you.

Drawing Your Heart

This heart meditation is one I often do when I am traveling or having a bad day, or just when I have a moment and want to remember it. If I am not in a place where I can draw, I imagine myself drawing it in my mind to memorize the images and perhaps later put them to paper.

Visualize your light and bring your light into your heart.

Take your light now on a journey into your heart, going deeper and deeper.

Find something in your mind that constricts the energy at your heart.

See it as clearly as you can.

Notice what happens to your body when you do this.

What kinds of things make your energy constrict at your heart?

Look in your imagination for a picture or an image, a color, shape or form, a situation that makes your heart energy constrict and make a note of it.

Now imagine your light, pure light at your heart, and see your heart open with generosity and warmth.

Feel it open.

What happens to you when your heart opens?

Does your body change?

Now look for a picture or image, a color, shape, or form, a situation where you feel your heart energy open and make a note of it.

See the light and your open heart, and see your color or shape very, very clearly.

Feel this heart warmth and generosity.

Feel its openness.

Let it bring you to the beautiful quality of loving and compassion inside of you, to your own sense of inner peace.

Feel the peace filling your being, filling your whole body.

Now extending to the room you are in and out into the universe.

Draw the experience.

Draw your confined heart and your opened heart, paying attention to how it opens and to how it brings you peace.

Drawing Your Shadow

Visualize your light with your mind's eye.

Imagine yourself touching your light, feeling it, and getting familiar with it.

Take a good look at it in your mind.

Perhaps imagine yourself touching it, imagining its texture and weight.

See your light emanate from inside of you, and feel it all around you.

In your light is a shadow.

Notice what the shadow looks like.

Let yourself look very closely at your shadow.

This shadow holds a picture or experience of yourself, a part of yourself.

What shape does it have?

What color, form, presence?

Let yourself get familiar with your shadow form.

Do you recognize this figure from a particular time in your life? Or a particular situation?

What kind of space does your shadow live in?

Is it inside of your body or outside of it?

Look around and really let yourself see it.

Now as you let yourself get familiar with this form, with this part of yourself, speak to it.

Ask your shadow form to tell you something about yourself that it wants you to know.

Ask it also to tell you why it's there.

And what it needs from you.

And what it wants from you.

Now very gently (don't be afraid, or if you are afraid, use your white light to help you with your fear) give the shadow the part of you that it wants.

Let yourself be very clear about what it wants and how you give it to your shadow.

See what your shadow does with this part of you.

Make a note of what you have observed.

Draw your shadow.

Draw yourself giving it what it wants.

Summoning Your Spirit from the Shadow

Imagine your light.

Remember the first shadow meditation and see if now your experience of the light is different.

Be with your light in your mind's eye.

Let yourself see it clearly.

Touch it in your mind.

Now imagine this light all around you as well as within you.

Imagine that there is an additional light.

It is a beam of light rising all around you, as far up as you can imagine.

This light now also goes below you down in to the earth, as far down as you can imagine.

You feel really connected to the universe, with the light going through you, above you, below you and all around you.

The energy in your light is now flowing from above you and beneath you through your body and all around you.

Now imagine your inner spirit self in your shadow coming to you in your light.

What does your spirit self look like?

What is she doing?

Let your spirit self reveal herself to you.

Is she familiar?

Does she remind you of someone or something?

Make a note of what you see.

Your spirit self now brings you back in time and shows you the sense of wonder you felt as a child.

Take a few minutes to find this part of you.

See yourself as a child feeling this sense of wonder and joy.

Take your time to find it.

What is this like for you?

What are you doing?

Where are you?

How old are you?

What do you get from this child, this wondrous child-spirit part of you?

Where does this wondrous child part live inside of you in your everyday life?

Let her give you a message about your inner sense of wonder and your communication with the universe.

Now you see the part of you that you found earlier in shadow.

She's coming into focus in your mind's eye.

See this shadow there very clearly.

Imagine yourself on a journey on a country road.

Let your shadow self take you on this road.

Visualize yourself there.

Walking along on this road, notice each part of the way.

Notice what the road looks like.

Notice if it changes as you are proceeding.

How it is constructed?

Bring yourself to different points on your way.

See this road as a visual representation of the different phases of your life, beginning with your child self.

See where your road has taken you, as you began to get older.

Let yourself see the span of your life on this road.

Make a note of what your road looks like.

Now, in your mind's eye, draw a beam of light onto your road.

Take that beam of light back with you in time.

Back, back, back in time.

To a place where you find the source of your shadow self.

To the beginning when you first became aware of it.

See how it came into being.

How it became part of you, and how it evolved.

Why did this shadow part come to be part of you in the first place?

How old are you?

When did it first come into being?

What purpose did it serve in your life at this time?

What did it give you? Why?

Who put it there?

How did it help you?

Who did it help?

Now have your spirit self speak to this shadow part of you and make friends with it.

How can you do that?

What do you need to do?

Can you help it to understand how you and it can work together to heal you?

How can it give you clarity?

How can you make peace with it so that it no longer has to remain in a dark place within you, so that you and it can become comfortable with each other?

See your shadow form changing and coming out into the light, now becoming one with your spirit, your inner self, so that you and it are together one with the other.

Draw your shadow self and your inner spirit self, both separate and together.

Draw the path, and your shadow coming into the light.

If your shadow self has changed from the first meditation, draw it with this one and compare them.

How are they the same?

How are they different?

Finding the Light in the World Tree

> He went into the yard of his house, where there were a few trees, fig trees, olive trees…and he went one by one, embracing the trees and crying, saying goodbye to them because he knew he would not return. To see this, to live this, if that doesn't mark you for the rest of your life you have no feeling.
> —*Interview with Jose Saramago, Nobel laureate*
> *in literature, speaking of his ill grandfather*

I love this meditation, especially since I am a woodcarver. It is adapted from the ancient belief found in many cultures that trees embody the sacred. In the Hebrew Kabbalah the symbolism of "the tree of life" is used as a map to explain reality and is a metaphor to describe the spheres of the divine. I often find myself speaking to the tree in the wood in which I am carving, asking it to guide me on my journey with it.

Imagine your white light.

Bring it down through your body.

Visualize it inside of you.

Now focus this light at your third eye, the space between your eyebrows where your intuition resides.

Stay there for a moment with your light and breathe and breathe.

Imagine a cave with your mind's eye.

Imagine yourself entering the cave.

It is very dark inside.

Get used to the darkness in your mind.

You go farther and farther into the cave seeing only darkness.

You continue in the cave until you come to an opening deep inside.

There is a ladder at the opening.

Begin to climb it.

You go up each step, little by little until you reach the top.

It is dark and still inside, very dark, but your eyes are getting used to the darkness.

Stay quietly in this new place.

As your eyes adjust you see that you are inside of a tree, a very large tree.

You have climbed up into a tree.

The tree invites you to go further inside it.

Become familiar with what it is like to be inside of and with the energy of the tree.

Feel its connection to nature.

Feel its inner power and spirit.

Look around you.

Are you alone?

Is there anyone else there?

Now let the tree itself guide.

Notice its inner structure, its core.

Let yourself get to know it.

The tree brings you up to its branches and leaves, and you climb higher.

You see yourself now outside the tree.

The tree gives you a place to stand on its branches.

You are standing on a large branch.

See what this place looks like.

What are the branches like?

What kind of tree is it?

Do you know it from before?

Let yourself take the time to experience standing here.

You are here as the great spirit of the universe.

Let yourself experience the spirit light as you become the great shaman (the wise woman or man).

Open your arms and embrace everything around you.

Call one of the wise spirits to come.

It is the spirit of newness, of spring, that comes to you.

It is the spirit of awakening, of opening.

Let the spirit appear to you.

Watch her stand before you.

What does your spirit look like?

Take a good look.

Now ask your spirit to tell you something it would like you to know about yourself.

Pay attention.

Let it tell you.

Make a note of it.

Bring your light back through your body with your breath.

Take it to your third eye. (This is located midway between your eyebrows and it is the center of your intuition and psychic sight.)

Stay there for a few minutes.

Now open your eyes and draw, paint, or collage what you have seen.

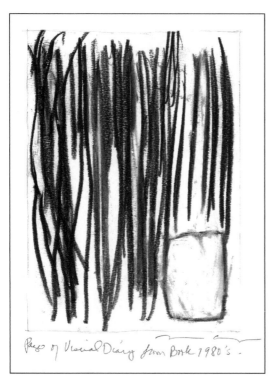

Page of Visual Diary from Book 1980's.

ITALIAN DOG

There is a dog nearby, locked into an untended, unruly garden. He is large and predominately white with black and gray spots. He is an expensive breed of dog, probably of the same breed as my friend Jane's dog. He is very lovely to watch from here, from my deck at the hotel, as he paces in the garden all day long. I often hear him whimper and cry throughout the day. He is lonely for someone and doesn't want to be without them, I think. He also amuses himself by howling with the church bells at different times during the quarter hour cycle of incessant ringing. He is a good-looking but neglected dog. Yesterday, as I was on my balcony, I saw him slide around the barricade in the garden and run loose. I became worried for him in his freedom and wondered what dangers lay ahead for him roaming about Assisi all alone. I comforted myself with the fact that Assisi is a small town and that whoever found him would return him, but I still had great fear that he was lost. I found that the dog returned in my dream last night; it escaped in the dream too and was lost. It felt like all of that freedom was too much for him, and he didn't know what to do with it. He was lost in his freedom and needed a support, a guide post that showed the way, a place that brought him some structure, some safety.

10

Gardens for the Spirit

He does not desire the soul to undertake any labor, but only to
take delight in the first fragrance of the flowers...the soul can
obtain sufficient nourishment from its own garden.

ST. THERESA OF AVILA

There is a new garden in my Tribeca neighborhood. For many years
it was a triangular patch of concrete, and now the triangular patch is
filled with blooms. As I am writing this it is August, and every morning, when I walk my dogs, it makes me so happy to take them there
and visit with the garden. I feel refreshed and inspired as I walk among
the black-eyed Susans, begonias, roses, and all of the greenery.

   This selection of five meditations always brings me to the different gardens, fields, and forests I have known and loved over the
years.

The Garden That Speaks to You

Find your special place and sit comfortably there, bringing your
light through your body with your breath.

Now visualize your light outside of you.

Spend a moment there and watch with your mind's eye the light
as it is outside of you.

It is very early in the day.

You are in the light of very early morning.

Imagine a stone fence with a gate.

Put yourself in a picture with the fence, and imagine yourself walking toward it.

Take a good look at it.

Open the gate on the fence.

Notice how you enter it.

What does the entrance gate look like?

What it is made out of?

What kind of door does it have?

What kind of latch?

Take a good look.

You now see in front of you a beautiful old path.

Enter onto the path.

Begin to walk on it.

Let yourself get comfortable on it.

The sun is rising.

You feel comfortable with yourself as you experience the early morning air.

You watch the light filter through the bushes and plants of your garden onto your path.

The birds are beginning to sing, and they share their song with you.

Listen carefully to their song.

What is it like? Do you recognize it?

Have you heard it before?

You look ahead of you.

You see that you are at the edge of a large English garden with its carefully planned flowers and foliage, colors and shapes neatly tucked into rows and circles.

Enter your garden.

Look around in it.

Notice ivy on the sides of the stone walls.

Walk around your garden.

Experience the fragrance

> Of jasmine

> Of lilacs

> And many other flowers in the early morning air.

Vivid colors and scents of your flowers are all around you in your garden.

Continue to walk further on the path.

There are many shadows.

Long shadows of the plants reflect onto the path.

You see the shadows of the tall iris,

> Shadows of the rows of sweet peas and pansies, of lavender and the mint,

> Shadows of thyme, which is very bushy and fragrant,

> And of sage, which is silvery green.

As you continue, you stop by six azalea bushes of different colors,

Of reds and purples and whites.

Spend a moment with them.

There are now rows of lilies, lilies of the valley, tiger lilies and white lilies.

Spend time with them.

Ask if they will give you a message for your spirit.

What do they tell you?

You continue to walk along.

In front of you is a large circle of roses.

Walk into your rose garden.

This, your rose garden, represents your spiritual awareness.

It is encircled by white roses with pink-tipped petals.

Stay there for a few minutes.

Let yourself become part of the garden.

Notice the red and yellow roses.

Near the center, the pretty pink ones are opening their flowers toward you.

Become more and more part of your garden.

Get to know your rose garden.

Become very familiar with it.

Continuing on your path, you come upon a bench with a water fountain in front of it.

You sit down at the bench and rest there.

Let yourself experience the pleasure that comes to you from sitting in your garden.

Look over it with your mind.

It is an important part of your spirit to sit in your garden.

Sitting there gives you a sense of inner strength, of inner wisdom.

As you sit there, you learn more about your spirit.

Note it in your mind as clearly as you can.

Draw your garden, the flowers in it, the fountain, the bench.

Draw your spirit.

The Open Field

Walk down the path to an open field of wildflowers.

Look around at the wildflowers.

See their beauty and their untamed exuberance.

The sun is now up in your morning field.

Your wildflowers are sparkling in the sunlight.

You see daisies and poppies and dandelions.

A cushion of dense grass is very soft under foot.

You lie down in the field and let the gentle morning sun warm you, paying attention to how you feel with the sun on your face and skin.

You feel its warmth and you experience the power and energy of its light for you.

Your field is a spacious, open place for you.

What is in your field that needs to be resolved?

What does it tell you?

Make a note of it what it tells you.

The Wild Forest

You now walk on farther to a forest.

This forest has a wildness to it that you recognize in yourself.

It is beautiful and overgrown with many plants and bushes, the wild things in your life.

As you walk through the forest you see many wildflowers and bushes.

You see juniper berries and healing flowers, goldenseal, echinacea, and large and small pines.

You find a rock and you sit on it

Let yourself relax with it, experiencing the overgrowth of the forest and the intermingling of one plant with the other.

Stay on the rock.

Stay and listen.

Feel the sensations that come to you on the rock.

This forest has a message for you about yourself, about your spirit.

Listen for it.

Make a note of what it tells you.

Draw the forest, the plants, the rock.

Draw your spirit.

Returning to your Path

Then you start back from the forest.

Walk through the field to your path, paying attention to what happens.

As you go back, you let your mind's eye find a place for you.

This is a special place, your place.

Where your spirit can grow.

Look over this place.

Become familiar with it.

Notice special places on your path

    And in the forest

    And in the garden

    And in the field.

Let these special places tell you why they want to be with you,

How it is connected to you.

Make a note of all this.

Draw your experience.

What gave you messages?

What you would like to know more about?

See if you can imagine yourself becoming each flower as you draw it.

Finding Your Special Plant

There is a special plant in your garden, field or forest.

Look around in your imagination to find it.

This plant wants you to give it special nurturing and attention.

It is a plant that has a history for you.

It has a past that is necessary for you to understand, to resolve, come to terms with.

To get to know.

It represents a part of your spirit that is calling you.

What is your plant like?

Take a good look at it.

How is it growing?

What is around it?

What kind of leaves does it have?

What colors does it have?

How tall is it?

How wide is it?

What is it about this plant that has a special connection to you?

What kind of history does it have?

What part of your spirit is calling you with this plant?

What part of your spirit wants you to pay attention to it with its message?

Become the plant.

Gently become your plant.

How old are you as the plant?

What are you doing?

What other people are there?

See what this plant represents to you.

What do you need to know about it?

About yourself?

Let it bring you to your spirit.

Let it tell you why it has come to you today.

What does it want you to know about yourself?

Now see your spirit plant telling you how to complete the unresolved or unknown parts that the plant represents.

Put those parts back into your life. Heal them.

How does your spirit self tell you to heal them?

In what way do you receive nutriment from this plant?

How do you give it the attention that it needs?

Let your spirit self share the direction of your future with your plant.

Take this nurturing and healing, whatever needs to be healed,

And go into the direction of your future with it.

See what you need to do.

Stay with your plant.

Become familiar with it.

Now draw your plant.

Draw yourself as the plant and as what is unresolved.

Draw the direction of yourself for your future.

Draw yourself applying these experiences to your life now and in the future.

LOOKING AT THE MOON

I look at the moon and see its profile. I could fly up to it and hold myself in it. Wrapped in the moon, held in place. Could I capture the moon for myself even for a moment, I wonder? Hang on to the moon, swing on its curve? Dance on the moon. Moon magic in the light of the moon, moonlight, shadow of the moon.

You were pretty last night. You were in fact transparent and did shine over anything and everything. You looked down and saw it all, wise moon. I am remembering that Tevye story about you that I heard so long ago. About the men who were trying to capture the full moon in a bucket of water. It's been so long since I heard it, but I think several of them got together and moved a barrel around until it caught the reflection of the moon and then covered the barrel tightly. The next day they uncovered the barrel, look inside, and found that the moon's reflection was gone. The golden moon being found and chased, then quickly captured and covered. The assurance that it could be caught, held in place. Theirs, now and forever.

11

Opening the Heart toward Loving Kindness

Where do we begin? Begin with the heart.

JULIAN OF NORWICH, FOURTEENTH-CENTURY
CHRISTIAN MYSTIC

Several years ago, I made a small sculpture about St. Theresa of Avila, a valentine for her, called *Seven Mansions*. The title was inspired by her book, *Interior Castle*. Made from a cross section of a tree with a carved red wood jewel form at the center, the sculpture has a twine-wrapped branch intersecting this jewel and two sparkling golden wings of wood caressing the center, a heart of wings.

Consider how the language of the heart is a metaphor for many states and emotions. A good exercise is to try to visualize some of these words and phrases, to give them a presence by describing them visually on paper.

Beating heart	Heart shut down	Hearty
Big-hearted	Heart song	Heavy heart
Black heart	Heartbeat	Hungry heart
Empty heart	Heartless	Lighthearted
Happy heart	Heartrending	Openhearted
Heartfelt	Heartsick	Pure-hearted
Heart of gold	Heartwarming	Sad heart

This six-part heart meditation is designed to explore a sense of lovingness, empathy, and compassion for ourselves and to help you develop a capacity for sharing this openheartedness with others. Bring this experience of self to your artwork. This series of meditations can be done daily, weekly, or as you choose.

Draw Your Heart

Imagine your heart at the center of yourself.

Take a picture of your heart there.

This picture can be your heart literally or a metaphorical reference to your heart.

Let this picture speak to you.

Let it tell you something about yourself.

Draw your heart.

The Mystic Dance of Life

Imagine a drumbeat.

Listen for it in the silence of your body.

You are at the beginning of a path to your heart.

Imagine your inner light.

Now visualize your inner light going through your being and breathe with it.

Breathe and relax, breathe and relax.

This path is of stones and branches.

You walk on it toward the place of loving kindness within you.

It is a long narrow path, and it is dark.

There is a light far in the distance that you can see from your path.

It is quiet except for the sound of your heartbeat in the silent darkness.

Let yourself become used to the darkness.

Listen to the sound of your heartbeat (the Egyptians called this beat the mystic dance of life).

Walk on this path to your heart.

What are you like here?

Who is there?

Take a moment to notice.

How old you are on the path?

What are you doing?

What are you wearing?

How does your heart feel inside of you as you are walking on the path?

Walk through this path to find the entrance to your heart.

Hear the beat of your heart in your silence.

See the pattern of your path below your feet.

Hear the beat of your heart.

What is this path like below your feet?

What is this path like that is leading you to your heart?

Your feet move in the pattern of your heartbeat.

The rhythm of the sound brings you closer to a light that is way off in the distance.

You look around and see a man to your left and a woman to your right.

The sound of your own heartbeat continues with the sound of your breath.

Breathing, breathing.

Notice the rhythm of your breath and your heartbeat. Just quietly note it.

Now take a look at the man.

What does he look like?

What does he represent for you?

He tells you something about yourself.

What does he say?

Who is he?

What does he want you to know?

What can he tell you about yourself?

Make a note of it.

Now take a look at the woman.

What does she look like?

What does she represent for you of your heart self?

She tells you something about yourself.

What does she say?

What does she want you to know?

What can she tell you about yourself?

Make a note of it.

As you are looking and listening with them, you notice something about yourself.

You notice your age and your manner.

You see the clothes you are wearing.

Notice if they are different from before.

Now draw the path, the man and woman.

Looking at Your Heart

Imagine the drum inspired by the sound of your heartbeat.

Bring your light into your body, releasing tension and relaxing yourself.

You will now continue on the path toward loving kindness.

Your inner light shines on you,

Within you,

Outside of you.

Hear your heartbeat.

Follow it with your mind and breath.

You now go toward the light.

It is leading you to the center, the focus of your universe,

Your own heart,

The place of the mystic dance of your own life.

Visualize your own life's blood within you, how it flows.

Spend a moment there, traveling with it.

Listen to your breath and hear the sound of your heart.

Listen closely.

The breath and the sound of your heart are close together.

You can feel yourself approaching this center.

Look at your path and notice even more clearly how it is shaped.

Is it different from the earlier meditation?

If so, how has it changed?

What is different about it?

Now continue to walk and walk and walk even more until you come to a gate in the path toward your heart.

This gate is transparent in places.

You can look through it and see the beating of your heart.

See yourself standing there.

Now take a good look at yourself in this picture.

How old are you?

What are you wearing?

Are there others at the entrance of your gate?

Are they with you?

Who are they?

What do they look like?

Now stand in front of your gate.

How big is it?

What is it made out of?

How thick is it?

How can you open it?

What holds it shut?

Look around and get a good look at your gate.

Is it locked?

How can you open it?

Is there a latch, a lock?

Find a way to open this gate to your heart.

You enter.

What is it you see there?

What is it like to see your heart from the entrance to your gate?

Who is there at your heart?

What is the color of your heart?

Draw your path as it is now,

Your gate, the entrance to your gate,

And your heart as you see it there.

Dropping the Barrier

Hear your heartbeat.

Imagine the sound of your heartbeat as the voice of your heart within you.

Listen carefully.

Imagine your inner light and return to your gate.

Enter through your gate and notice if it is different from before.

You are now inside of your gate.

What does it look like now?

See your heart from the entrance.

Begin to approach it.

Slowly walk toward it.

Notice if there is anything on this interior path that is important for you to see.

Look down.

Has the path changed?

What kind of shape and form does it have?

How big is it now?

How wide?

How different?

What colors do you see there on this path going toward your heart?

Continuing on the path approaching your heart, you get closer and closer.

You see your heart enclosed inside a barrier.

What does the barrier look like?

How does this barrier surround your heart?

What is it made out of?

What color and design is it?

It tries to protect your heart from being wounded.

How does it do that?

Is the barrier connected in some way to the gate?

How is it different?

How is it the same?

Now look at your heart.

Ask your heart for permission to pass through this barrier or to have it dropped.

Ask permission to go into it.

Your heart tells you what to do and encourages you to go behind the barrier.

Look around and see if you recognize this barrier.

Is it familiar?

Do you connect it to somewhere, to something?

When did it first come to be part of your heart?

How old were you when this happened?

What were you doing?

Make a note of it.

Now you see the chambers of your heart.

Around them are all the scars from wounds to your heart.

Imagine the scars and wounds.

What do they look like?

How do they reside at your heart?

What happened in your life to make these wounds?

Take your time.

How old were you?

Find the situation(s).

See them.

Let yourself use your inner light to help you with them.

Who wounded you?

How did that happen?

Draw your heart, your barrier, your wounds.

Healing the Heart

Go back to your heart on the path.

Enter through your gate and visit the part of your heart that is wounded and scarred.

Bathe it in white light, a healing white light, filling the wounds with this healing light.

Stay with the light for a moment.

Go deeper into your heart.

Find the space that holds the memory of the people and things that you love.

Let your inner self move deeper and deeper into your heart.

See what your path is like as you do.

How do you arrive there?

You are getting closer and closer to your heartbeat.

Imagine that happening with your mind's eye.

Feel your heartbeat and your breath coming together, as you get closer and closer and deeper and deeper.

You hear the sound of your heartbeat.

Feel its power.

It becomes music to you.

The rhythm of the sound is your breath.

Breathe and breathe.

Now look around at this place deep within your heart.

What does this place look like?

This place of your tender, openhearted, loving self.

Look around.

Do you recognize it?

What is it made of?

How big is it?

Do you recognize it?

Now see the people whom you love and who love you, deep in this space.

Take a few moments and carefully look.

Who are they?

Go to each one and visit with them, talk to them.

Feel your love radiating with them.

What would they like to tell you about yourself?

What would they like you to know about your sense of loving and being loved?

Now go very deep into the center of your heart.

Find the part of you that has been sleeping for many years.

Bring it together with your loving part and your scarred part.

See all three together.

What has your sleeping part been like?

Why has it been asleep?

What does it look like?

See if you can get a picture of it.

Let it talk to you.

Now imagine your heart becoming awake, your awakened heart.

Visualize in your mind the mystic dance of your heartbeat.

Imagine a red stone, carnelian, garnet, or ruby that represents your heart.

Let this stone be an amulet for you.

Bring your light to the center of your heart.

Let it rest there for a moment.

Draw your heart as it was when you began this meditation.

Now draw your awakened heart, your sleeping heart, your scarred heart, and the amulet at your heart.

Awakening Love and Compassion

Bring your light to your heart and hear your heart beat.

Listen to the musical sound of your breath.

Go back to your heart path and imagine it now.

See your scars and wounds and fill them with white light.

See your loved ones and fill them with white light.

Let the white light radiate on you and on your heart.

See the light just shining down on your heart.

Now go deep into the center of your heart.

Find that place within you.

What does the deep center of your heart look like?

What is there?

What are the walls, the floor, and the ceiling like?

Spend a moment there watching your heart from this deep inside place.

Look around inside and find the place in your heart where your sense of loving and compassion has been asleep.

What does this sleeping part of your heart look like?

How long has it has been asleep, for how many years?

How will you awaken it?

Ask it why it has been sleeping.

What has been inside of your heart to keep it asleep all of these years?

What has held it back from being connected to you?

Bring it out into the light.

Look at it bathed in white light.

See how the light that bathes it opens and awakens this part of you.

Prepare for a dance in your heart, a dance of light.

See yourself preparing for the dance.

How old are you?

What are you doing?

What are you wearing?

Bring this part of you into preparation for your dance.

What do you need to wear to do this?

Let yourself put it on.

Get all the things you need for your dance.

Now bring into your consciousness the different parts of your heart:

> The scarred and wounded part of yourself,
>
> The loving and loved part of yourself,
>
> And the newly awakened part of yourself.

See yourself preparing for the dance, entering into the dance of celebration for your heart.

Hear your heart beat for the music.

You are going deeper and deeper, closer to the essence of who you are.

You are getting closer to the center of the life force within you.

See the pattern and rhythm of the dance within you.

Watch how you move.

How does it feel?

Dancing and dancing.

Spinning and spinning.

Moving and moving.

Turning and turning.

Free and open, celebrating your heart and your life.

No longer asleep.

Your awakened heart is clear and open to you.

Awake, you dance to your red stone, the amulet of your dance.

You take the stone into your hand and put it to your heart.

Feel the power of your stone at your heart.

Dancing and dancing with this red stone at your heart.

Draw the experience.

Draw yourself dancing.

Draw your stone and your awakened heart.

JENNY

I didn't know either grandmother very well personally, but I could often watch Grandma Como, my mother's mother because she lived downstairs from us in the big house that we shared on the corner of Eleventh Avenue and 82nd Street in St. Bernadette's parish in Brooklyn.

Everyday, my mother would go downstairs to Grandma's apartment and my sister and I would have to come with her. As my mother and grandmother would talk away, I would examine the surroundings. There were many things to look at and to touch. Some were in a glass cabinet that held little painted china slippers stuffed with white almonds and wrapped in bridal tulle and souvenirs from family weddings. Others, like an incense burner of green glass, stood on a table and had a little wick that smelled good. There was a green, overstuffed sofa with many cushions to play with and a pink and rose Persian rug to lie on and designs to trace with my finger, or curl my body around.

Sometimes when they were getting ready to go out, Grandma would pull herself into her corset and I would stand by the door and watch in wonder. This "garment" as she called it was very odd to a child. It was the full length of her torso and it almost stood up on its own. It was pink and boned and had embroidery and little flowers woven into its delicate jacquard weave. I would be in awe as she put it around herself and worked the hooks and eyes on the front of it. When she was finished hooking, she put her hands on her waist and shook herself into it. I couldn't imagine how it would feel to shake myself into anything like that.

It seems so long ago; it is hard to trust the memories. Yet when I think of Grandma, I see her fresh and vivid in my mind with her flashing black eyes, her golden olive skin, her beautiful smile. I see her in her very white starched ruffled pinafore, fresh figs from the garden stuffed in her pockets, or holding her skirt dancing at weddings which she loved to do; or I see her in a green Adirondack lawn chair reading one of her "health books," as the family referred to them.

One summer day Grandma was standing on her rose and ivy covered porch with the green awning talking to her two sisters-in-law, Scia Nina and the other Scia. I could hear them speaking in Italian, the two aunts on the gentle porch swing talking in unison, Grandma responding. It was a striking picture, both aunts attired in black: stockings, shoes, sweaters, dresses, their gray hair pulled taut into a bun, stocky and somber. Grandma was not like them in her pastel silk print dress, her smart, white mesh shoes, her own gray hair cut and coiffed. She was a much more modern woman than her sisters-in-law and she had an intensity of the artist about her that drew her in different directions. When Uncle Frank went to chiropractic school, she read through his books. When he lost interest, she continued on her own and taught herself to give adjustments and to follow the recommended exercises and diet. She had this part of her that made her unique from everyone else in our neighborhood. Her studies made her a fervent believer in natural foods and exercise and as she extended this practice to her family, we children were perfect subjects for her.

On school days coming home I would walk up the stairs of our house—we lived upstairs, she downstairs—and I would tiptoe very slowly, very quietly, trying to slip by, but the stair would always creak, and Grandma would open her door and catch me. She would politely ask me to come in. There was no question of resistance, I had to go in. I would enter and stand very straight, close to the door, so I could make a quick exit as soon as she let me go. But Grandma had other things in mind. She would look at the palms of my hands first, look very closely, and then she would look at my nails to see if they were rough, if they had white spots. Were they pink enough? Then she would look at my eyes, gazing into them intently pulling the lids up and down, the whole time her mind working away, taking impressions. When she finished with this she ordered me to stick my tongue out and she would make her diagnosis. Carrots, spinach, celery, kale, chicory, all went into the juicer. I would shift my weight, from one foot to the other, edging closer to the door, but it was clear that I couldn't leave without having a glass of her juice. "Drink it," she would command, kind but no longer polite. She couldn't understand why I didn't appreciate her tonic, why I didn't greet it with enthusiasm, sure it was an elixir for our health, important for us to have.

My sister Victoria and I had dinner one night. I asked her if she remembered any of Grandma's recipes because I couldn't, and she said carrot juice. We both marveled. She didn't remember some special macaroni or a great fish dish; carrot juice is what came to her mind.

"She was way ahead of her time," Vicky said. "Grandma also did yoga." I hadn't remembered. I thought that it was calisthenics. "Don't you remember Grandma standing on her head?" she asked.

"She did? I've been trying to stand on my head in my yoga class for fifteen years and I still can't do it!" Then I remembered Grandma standing on her head in her living room, very serious and very straight and very accomplished.

When Jenny died at eighty-three, I made a sculpture for her. Named for her, Jenny Caputo Como, it is made from many pieces of carved oak, ash, and pine wood all assembled together. Grandma was spirited and curious, the only one I knew then who questioned and explored her life in ways that other women in her community did not. This clearly helped me find my way in life—to look beyond my family's expectations and become the person I am today.

12

Spirit Wheels

The Spiritual Warrior sits in the middle of the fire.

PEMA CHODRON

When I was a little girl, each year I waited with great excitement for the *festa*, the annual feast day of Bernadette, the saint of our parish. This celebration was like a fair with games and prizes. My favorite was the wheel of chance. The wheel, with its brightly colored numbers and symbols, was magical to me. Once engaged, it would spin so rapidly that my vision was blurred until the wheel stopped short at a number or a symbol. Sometimes, at the very last second, it would move ever so slightly to another number. I would be in suspense watching it, speculating on where it would stop and holding my breath in excitement.

There are so many different symbols of the wheel in our culture. There is the wheel of life, the wheel of fortune, the wheel of time. In other cultures there is the prayer wheel and the Hindu chakras, which means "wheel" in Sanskrit. These images and others, such as the carousel, the roulette, the Ferris wheel, and in particular the Native American Medicine Wheel, have inspired these meditations.

Finding Your Center

Let yourself relax.

Imagine your light going through your body.

Imagine your light centered at your heart.

Stay there with it for a moment.

Imagine movement around your heart.

Just focus on a feeling there.

Now visualize a wheel at your heart.

Imagine this wheel in motion.

Watch it in your mind and take a good look at it.

How large is it?

How does it move?

What color is it?

Your wheel has a center, a hub, a large rim, and eight spokes.

Four of those spokes are oriented to the cardinal points: north, east, south, and west.

Let your mind's eye bring you very close to it.

Let yourself feel as if you are the wheel itself.

Imagine that you become the wheel, your wheel.

You are it. It is you.

You have a center and you have a rim, and you are very strong.

You are stronger than you have ever been.

And you begin to move, and to move with it.

Gently go around all the parts of your inner self with a very slow, beautiful rotation.

What does your wheel look like?

What does your rim look like?

What is it made of?

What are your spokes like?

In your mind's eye, or your heart's eye, envision the center, the hub.

Take a good look.

Draw yourself on the wheel.

Spinning Wheel

Imagine entering your wheel and begin to feel yourself dancing and spinning around in it.

As you move around it, it moves around you, following your breath as you inhale and exhale in a wheel of energy.

You are yourself with your breath, becoming one with the wheel.

You are moving in a circle with your arms outstretched like a wheel.

You move in at the same speed as the wheel.

You are the wheel, and the wheel is you.

As you move with it, the wheel takes you back, back in time.

You are now a little child in a very old place, an ancient place.

You see the world with new eyes, with a child's eyes of wonder.

Find a time within your child self when you have these eyes of wonder and innocence.

Let yourself observe your self.

What is this ancient place like for you?

Is it familiar?

Look around at it.

What are you looking at?

Who else is there?

What are you doing?

Take a good look at yourself.

Place your child of wonder and innocence somewhere on your wheel.

Make a note of where the child is on your wheel.

Now again imagine your child in her ancient place.

Let yourself feel the experience of this child and see the wonder gone.

The child is lost and abandoned.

All around her is darkness, emptiness.

You are this child.

Let yourself feel what she feels.

What is all around her?

Let her feel her darkness, her emptiness.

How did she get there?

What happened to put her there?

Ask this child what she needs from you, what she wants you to give her.

How she can be less afraid of the darkness, be more familiar with it?

Now place this lost child, this part of yourself, on the wheel.

Return to your child self of wonder.

See yourself connecting to her.

Now see both child selves on your wheel.

Draw these children.

Singing Wheel

Your wheel is singing.

You hear it singing a prayer in the wind.

It spins and turns and moves with you.

Your wheel spins around as the sun rises, and around as the moon fades in the background.

See your wheel with your prayer on it and your body on it.

This is the wheel of life with the cycles and patterns of your existence.

You watch the wheel move and move and as you enter it, you become a newborn baby.

You are small and new.

You look around you.

You see your baby self, your baby face quite clearly, beautiful and clear and joyous.

Now ask her to tell you something about yourself.

Find a place for your baby on your wheel.

You now see yourself at a time in your childhood that was significant for you.

What is happening?

What are you doing?

Who is there?

What would your child self like you to know about this situation?

Put this child self on the wheel.

You are now getting into your teens.

Let your mind's eye take you to an important place in your adolescence.

See yourself there at a time that was important for you.

What are you doing?

Who is there?

What information about this time is there for you?

Listen carefully to everything that your teenage self tells you.

Place your teenage self somewhere on your wheel.

Now you see yourself as an adult.

Find an important place there.

What are you doing?

Who is there with you?

What would your adult self like to tell you?

Place your adult self on the wheel.

Now you see yourself as an old person, well into the future.

Where are you?

What are you doing?

How do you look?

What do you, the older person, want you—the you of right now—to know?

What message do you have for yourself as you are now?

Now put yourself in old age on your wheel.

Look at your different selves, from their different times, who are on the wheel.

Draw them.

Clear Light Wheel

You see in the distance eight distinct figures.

They are different parts of yourself.

These figures are far, far away in a forest among the trees.

They are in darkness.

They are calling you.

You hear their voices.

They represent the eight spokes of your wheel, the eight-pointed star.

As you approach, your figures begin to come out of the shadows.

You are able to see them more clearly.

The first figure is your fear coming out of the shadow. It is walking toward you.

What shape and form does it have?

What does your fear look like?

What kind of presence does it have?

What is familiar about it?

What is strange or different about it?

What does your fear want you to know about yourself?

Become familiar with it.

Can you befriend it?

What message does it have for you?

Place your figure of fear on the wheel.

The second figure that comes out of the dark is your fury, your rage.

At first it looks calm and quiet, but as it gets closer to you and the figure becomes clearer, you begin to see your rage for what it is.

What does your rage look like?

What shape and color and form does it have?

What does it want you to know about it?

Place it on your wheel.

The third figure is deeper in shadow and very well hidden.

It has several layers of cloth over it.

As it begins to move toward you, you see that it is your hatred.

Take a good look at what your hatred looks like.

About whom have you felt this way in your life?

What color, shape, and form does it have?

Who are your enemies? What are they like?

See your figure clearly and place it on your wheel.

Now you move farther into your shadows.

Deep in those recesses your jealousy is hidden.

You want to have, you are grasping, you want everything that someone else has.

What do you want?

Let yourself take a good look at it.

What does it look like?

Give it what it wants.

What happens when you give it everything it wants?

Now see your figure clearly and put it on your wheel.

The fifth figure you see is your despair.

Your figure of despair is lying on the ground, filled with emptiness.

It is lost and abandoned.

What does your figure of despair look like?

What shape and form does it have?

What color does your figure of despair have?

What does it want you to know about it?

Now put your figure of despair on your wheel.

As you watch the shadows and darkness, three figures emerge and become filled with the rainbow colors, bright and full.

They begin to glow.

The first figure is clarity of vision. It is in a beautiful clear light.

The clarity of vision holds openness and loyalty for you.

It comes to you and gives you the gift of clear vision.

You take your gift and put it with your figures on your wheel.

The next figure comes to you.

It is hope.

It is expansive, clear, and beautiful, and it contains all the things you would wish to have and be.

It is broad, full, and wonderful.

What do you hope for yourself?

See what they are, each one of them.

Now put your hopes on your wheel.

The last figure, which is the most radiant and glowing, is the figure of your love, your compassion, and your joy.

What does this figure look like?

Let it come to you and speak to you.

What does your love and compassion want you to know?

Now see yourself filled with the joy of your inner life.

As you feel this joy flooding through you, put your figure of love and compassion on your wheel.

Now see all eight figures.

See the figures of fear, rage, hatred, jealousy, and despair.

See clarity bathed in the light of clarity and vision.

See hope.

See love and compassion and joy.

See the eight spokes of your wheel all together and draw them.

Now see how they look on your page.

Where have you placed them?

How do they relate to each other and to yourself in this illustration?

Sacred Wheel

Watch all your spokes moving with the wheel, around and around.

The spinning spokes lead you to your heart.

See yourself at your heart in the center of your wheel, spinning and spinning and spinning and spinning.

It now lets you go.

You begin to drop into the center, spinning farther and farther down until your whole being is brought deep into the core of the center.

Here you are at the vortex.

You are at Mt. Meru, the great sacred mountain in the center of the earth.

The mountain is made totally of crystal.

It is the most beautiful and sacred thing that you have ever seen.

Its light is luminous and sparkling like a mountain of pure ice.

There is a great all-seeing eye at the center of the crystal.

As you begin to climb to reach the eye, you see a mirror image of yourself, beautiful and radiant, filled with the experience of ecstasy.

Each step takes you closer to the essence of your inner self.

You now hear your prayer as it spins in the wind, and it has new meaning for you as it moves around you.

Light, pure joy, pure ecstasy, pure oneness with your inner life.

Your prayer restores you, brings your life to an internal balance, connecting you to eternity, to what always was, and to what always will be.

Watch how your inner self restores you to balance.

What is it you need in your life that your inner self is now able to give you?

How will the changes be made?

What can you do, what will you do, to give your life that pure light, pure joy?

Draw this light and joy.

Flying to the Sun of Unconditional Love

Bring your light to your heart and let it rest there for a moment.

You are now going to fly into the sun like Icarus from Greek mythology, but your wings won't melt.

Stay with the light at your heart for a moment.

Notice your heart beat.

Sense your blood flowing through your body.

Imagine yourself finding a pair of wings for yourself for your journey.

Look over in your mind the many different varieties of birds.

Decide which bird has the pair of wings that you would like to borrow.

Spend some time doing this.

When you have decided which bird to choose, ask permission from this bird to borrow her wings.

Take her wings and begin to prepare for your journey.

Look over your wings for safety and strap them on.

How do they feel?

How do they fit you?

Now find a high place of your choice to fly off on your journey.

Very slowly at first, fly into the sunlight, feeling the air around you.

Look at the ground beneath you.

Warmth and joy come over you, and you begin to soar into the sunlight, coasting or navigating with your wings as you need to.

Eventually, you rise toward the sun, which although bright, is welcoming to you.

After much traveling, you fly into the sun.

As you rest there, a beam of sunlight reveals to you a secret about unconditional love.

As you continue to feel its warmth and healing, you find a

symbol for yourself that represents this experience of unconditional love on your journey.

Be there with it.

What does your symbol look like?

How big is it?

What color is it?

How does it feel to hold it?

What is it about the secret of unconditional love that is in this symbol for you?

Allow yourself to spend some time learning about this secret for yourself.

Then take your symbol and put it under your wings carefully.

Secure it so that it doesn't fall during your journey back.

You now spend one last minute looking and absorbing this experience.

You begin to turn around for your flight back, your return to the high place of your choice.

You come back gradually, looking over the terrain, and eventually you land on your safe high place.

You now take off your wings and give them back to your bird as you thank her for her generosity.

Draw your bird.

Draw yourself strapped into her wings.

Draw your symbol of the secret of unconditional love.

Hang your drawing of your symbol in your workspace.

Refer to it often.

Yoga Prayer

Yoga teacher Carolyn Oberst adapted this prayer from her first yoga teacher, Swami Bua, many years ago. She recites it at the end of each class. I often find myself repeating it during the course of a day.

I am not this body.
I am not this mind.
I am not this spirit.
I am something supreme.
I am something divine.
I am something eternal.
Namaste *(The divine in me greets the divine in you.)*

Let your self guide you.

List of Artists

Romare Beardon, mixed media, American, 1912–1988

Joseph Beuys, sculptor, mixed media, German, 1921–1986

William Blake, artist, poet, English, 1757–1827

Pierre Bonnard, painter, French, 1867–1947

Louise Bourgeois, sculptor, American born in France, b.1911

Constantin Brancusi, sculptor, French born in Romania, 1876–1957

John Milton Cage, Jr., experimental composer, American, 1912–1992

Willem de Kooning, painter, American born in Holland, 1904–1997

Edwin Dickinson, painter, American, 1891–1978

Emily Dickinson, poet, American, 1830–1886

Adolph Gottlieb, painter, American, 1903–1974

El Greco, painter, Spanish born in Greece, 1541–1614

Giotto, painter, Italian, 1267–1337

Barbara Hepworth, sculptor, English, 1903–1975

Hildegard of Bingen, painter, author, abbess, German, 1098–1179

Anish Kapoor, sculptor, English born in India, b.1954

Anselm Kiefer, mixed media artist, German, b. 1945

Paul Klee, painter, Swiss, 1879–1940

René François Magritte, painter, Belgian, 1898–1967

Henri Matisse, painter, French, 1869–1954

Michelangelo, painter and sculptor, Italian, 1475–1564

Henry Moore, sculptor, English, 1898–1986

Robert Motherwell, painter, American, 1915–1991

Louise Nevelson, sculptor, American born in Russia, 1899–1988

Georgia O'Keeffe, painter, American, 1887–1986

Meret Oppenheim, mixed media, Swiss German, 1913–1985

Octavio Paz, poet, writer, Mexican, 1914–1998

Pablo Picasso, painter, French born in Spain, 1881–1973

Jackson Pollock, painter, American, 1912–1956

Faith Ringgold, mixed media, American, b.1930

Auguste Rodin, sculptor, French, 1840–1917

Mark Rothko, painter, American born in Russia, 1903–1970

John Singer Sargent, painter, American, 1856–1925

Arnold Schoenberg, composer, Austrian, 1874–1951

Igor Stravinsky, composer, American born in Russia, 1882–1971

Margaret Tafoya, ceramic artist, Native American, 1909–2001

Lenore Tawney, mixed media and fiber artist, American, b. 1907

References and
Further Reading

Ackroyd, Peter. *Blake*. New York: Ballantine Books, 1995.

Acterberg, Jean. *Imagery in Healing: Shamanism in Modern Medicine*. Boston: Shambhala, 1985.

Baker, Richard. Introduction to *Zen Mind, Beginner's Mind* by Shunryu Suzuki. New York: John Weatherhill, Inc., 1970.

Baudelaire, Pierre Charles. *The Painter of Modern Life and Other Essays*. London: Phaidon Press, Ltd., 1964, 1995.

———. "The Queen of the Faculties." *In Art and Theory 1815–1900* by Charles Harrison, Paul Wood, and Jason Gaiger, eds. Malden, MA: Blackwell Publishers, 2001.

Berenson-Perkins, Janet. *Kabbalah Decoder*. Hauppauge, NY: Barrons, 2000.

Bloom, Pamela. *Buddhist Acts of Compassion*. Berkeley, CA: Conrai Press, 2000.

Budge, E. A. Wallis. *Egyptian Magic*. New York: Dover Publications, 1971.

Buber, Martin. *I and Thou*. New York: Scribner, 1974.

Cage, John. *Silence*. Middleton, CT: Wesleyan University Press, 1973.

Chipp, Hershel B. *Theories of Modern Art*. Berkeley, CA: University of California Press, 1968.

Chodron, Pema. *Start Where You Are*. Boston: Shambhala Press, 1994.

Cook, Roger. *The Tree of Life*. New York: Thames and Hudson, 1974.

Curiger, Bice. *Meret Oppenheim*. Zurich: Parkett Publishers, 1989.

Doyle, Brendan. *Meditations with Julian of Norwich*. Santa Fe: NM: Bear and Company, 1983.

Erickson, Erik. *Childhood and Society*. Reissued edition, New York: W. W. Norton and Company, 1993.

Fox, Matthew. *Illuminations of Hildegard of Bingen*. Santa Fe, NM: Bear and Company, 1985.

Halifax, Joan. *Shamanic Voices: A Survey of Visionary Narratives* New York: E. P. Dutton, 1979.

Hanh, Thich Nhat. *The Blooming of a Lotus*. Translated by Annabel Laity. Boston: Beacon Press, 1993.

———. *The Miracle of Mindfulness*. Translated by Mobi Ho. Boston: Beacon Press, 1975.

Harrison, Charles and Paul Wood, eds. *Art In Theory: 1900–1990*. New York and London: Blackwell Press, 1992.

Hepworth, Barbara. *Barbara Hepworth: A Pictorial Autobiography*. London: Tate Gallery Publications, 1985.

Huxley, Aldous. *The Art of Seeing*. Berkeley, CA: Creative Arts Book Company, 1982.

Johari, Harish. *Chakra: Energy Centers of Transformation*. Rochester, VT: Destiny Books, 1987.

Kandinsky, Wassily. *Conerning the Spiritual in Art*. Translated by M.T.H. Sadler. New York: Dover Publications, Inc., 1977.

Kornfield, Jack. *A Path With Heart: A Guide through the Perils and Promises of Spiritual Life*. New York: Bantam Books, 1993.

Kramrisch, Stella. *Unknown India: Ritual Art in Tribe and Village*. From a catalog of the Philadelphia Museum of Art, 1968.

Ma, Shri Anandi. *Divine Bliss, Sacred Songs of Devotion from the Heart of India*. From CD program notes for "Devotion." Boulder, CO: Sounds True, 1997.

Moore, Henry. *Henry Moore on Sculpture: Collection of the Sculptor's Writings and Spoken Words*. Introduction by Philip James. New York: The Viking Press, 1971.

Pagels, Elaine. *The Gnostic Gospels*. New York: Random House, 1979.

Pandit, M. P., ed. *Glossary of Sanskrit Terms in Sri Aurobindo's Works*. Ahmedabad: Sri Aurobindo Mandal, 1966.

Proust, Marcel. *Remembrance of Things Past*. Vol. 1, *Swann's Way*. Translated by Moncrieff and Kilmartin. New York: Vintage Books, 1982.

Purce, Jill. *The Mystic Spiral: Journey of the Soul*. New York: Avon Publishers, 1974.

Rinpoche, Sogyal. *The Tibetan Book of Living and Dying*. San Francisco: HarperSanFrancisco, 1992.

Rodin, Auguste. *Art*. Boston: Small, Maynard and Co., 1912.

Rothko, Mark. "The American Avant-Garde." In *Art in Theory: 1900–1990* by Charles Harrison and Paul Wood. New York and London: Blackwell Press, 1992.

Ruskin, John. *Lectures on Art*. New York: Allworth Press, 1996.

Saint Teresa of Avila. *Interior Castle*. Translated and edited by E. Allison Peers. New York: Image Books, 1989.

———. *The Life of Teresa of Jesus*. Translated by E. Allison Peers. New York: Image Books, 1960.

Shafton, Anthony M. *Dream Reader: Contemporary Approaches to the Understanding of Dreams*. New York: State University of New York Press, 1995.

Shane, John, ed. *The Crystal and the Way of Light: Sutra, Tantra, and Dzogchen*. New York and London: Routledge and Kegan Paul, 1986.

Sivananda, Sri Swami. *Yoga Vedanta Dictionary*. Dehli: Motilal Banarsidass, 1973.

Stokstad, Marilyn. *Art History*. Upper Saddle River, N.J.: Prentice Hall, 2002.

Storm, Hyemeyohsts. *Seven Arrows*. New York: Ballantine Books, 1972.

Stravinsky, Igor. *Igor Stravinsky, An Autobiography*. New York: W. W. Norton and Company, 1936.

Suzuki, Shunryu. *Zen Mind, Beginner's Mind*. New York: John Weatherhill, Inc., 1970.

Todd, Mabel Loomis and T. W. Higginson, eds. *Collected Poems of Emily Dickinson*. New York: Gramercy Books, 1982.

Trungpa, Chogyam. *Cutting Through Spiritual Materialism*. Berkeley, CA: Shambala Publications, Inc, 1973.

————. Visual Dharma: *The Buddhist Art of Tibet*. Berkeley, CA, and London: Shambala Press, 1975.

————. *Meditation in Action*. Boulder, CO: Shambala Press, 1969.

Vargiu, James. "Creativity." *Synthesis 3–4: The Realization of the Self*. Ed. Roberto Assagioli et al. Redwood City, CA: The Synthesis Press, 1977.

Vogel, Susan and Francine N'Diaye. *African Masterpieces*. New York: The Center for African Art and Abrams, 1985.

Walker, Barbara. *The Woman's Encyclopedia of Myths and Secrets*. San Francisco: Harper & Row, 1983.

Weisberger, Edward, ed. *The Spiritual In Art: Abstract Painting 1890–1985*. New York: Abbeville Press, 1986.

About the Author

Nancy Azara is a sculptor who has been teaching for thirty-five years. Her sculpture has been widely reviewed in such publications as the *New York Times, Art In America, Art Forum,* and *Sculpture Magazine* and has been exhibited widely in the United States and in Europe. She has traveled extensively and was an artist in residence in Kerala, India in 2002. She is the recipient of the Adolph and Esther Gottlieb Foundation Grant, the Susan B. Anthony Award, and most recently, a Bogliasco Foundation Fellowship. Nancy came of age during the feminist movement of the 1960s and began a lifelong spiritual practice that has influenced her art and led her to teach and perform psychic healing circles. In *Spirit Taking Form*, she marries both interests.